R. A.

Performance-Based Project
Management^{SM}

Performance-Based Project Management^{SM}

Increasing the Probability of Project Success

GLEN B. ALLEMAN

AMERICAN MANAGEMENT ASSOCIATION

New York • Atlanta • Brussels • Chicago • Mexico City • San Francisco
Shanghai • Tokyo • Toronto • Washington, D.C.

Bulk discounts available. For details visit:
www.amacombooks.org/go/specialsales
Or contact special sales:
Phone: 800-250-5308
Email: specialsls@amanet.org
View all the AMACOM titles at: www.amacombooks.org
American Management Association: www.amanet.org

This publication is designed to provide accurate and authoritative information in regard to the subject matter covered. It is sold with the understanding that the publisher is not engaged in rendering legal, accounting, or other professional service. If legal advice or other expert assistance is required, the services of a competent professional person should be sought.

"PMI" and the PMI logo are service and trademarks of the Project Management Institute, Inc. which are registered in the United States of America and other nations; "PMP" and the PMP logo are certification marks of the Project Management Institute, Inc. which are registered in the United States of America and other nations; "PMBOK", "PM Network", and "PMI Today" are trademarks of the Project Management Institute, Inc. which are registered in the United States of America and other nations; ". . . building professionalism in project management . . ." is a trade and service mark of the Project Management Institute, Inc. which is registered in the United States of America and other nations; and the Project Management Journal logo is a trademarks of the Project Management Institute, Inc.

PMI did not participate in the development of this publication and has not reviewed the content for accuracy. PMI does not endorse or otherwise sponsor this publication and makes no warranty, guarantee, or representation, expressed or implied, as to its accuracy or content. PMI does not have any financial interest in this publication, and has not contributed any financial resources.

Additionally, PMI makes no warranty, guarantee, or representation, express or implied, that the successful completion of any activity or program, or the use of any product or publication, designed to prepare candidates for the PMP® Certification Examination, will result in the completion or satisfaction of any PMP® Certification eligibility requirement or standard.

Performance-Based Project Management is a registered service mark of Niwot Ridge Consulting, LLC.

Library of Congress Cataloging-in-Publication Data

Alleman, Glen B.
  Performance-based project management : increasing the probability of project success / Glen B. Alleman.
    pages cm
  Includes bibliographical references and index.
  ISBN 978-0-8144-3330-0 (hardcover) — ISBN 0-8144-3330-8 (hardcover) — ISBN 978-0-8144-3331-7 (ebook)
  1. Project management. I. Title.
  HD69.P75A455 2014
  658.4'04—dc23

                                                                    2013038637

About AMA
American Management Association (www.amanet.org) is a world leader in talent development, advancing the skills of individuals to drive business success. Our mission is to support the goals of individuals and organizations through a complete range of products and services, including classroom and virtual seminars, webcasts, webinars, podcasts, conferences, corporate and government solutions, business books, and research. AMA's approach to improving performance combines experiential learning—learning through doing—with opportunities for ongoing professional growth at every step of one's career journey.

Printing number
10 9 8 7 6 5 4 3 2 1

To my wife, Linda B. Chartier, for her tireless
patience of my late night typing

CONTENTS

CHAPTER 2   **The Five Immutable Principles of Project Success**   **37**

CHAPTER 3   **The Five Immutable Practices of Project Success**   **65**

FIGURES

ACKNOWLEDGMENTS

This book is the result of my cumulative experience as a project and program manager and technical experience writing software for commercial, energy, space, and defense systems. These experiences have informed my thought processes over thirty years—some wonderful experiences, some not so wonderful. In the end, there are a small number of people who have caused me to rethink my view of the project management view of the world. The first is John Caterham, who was the CIO at Rocky Flats Environmental Technology Site in Golden, Colorado. Rocky Flats was a U.S. Department of Energy National Nuclear Security Agency production site from 1952 to 1992.

The cleanup of that site was what Edwin Land called *manifestly important and nearly impossible*. John led not only the IT department but also the removal of infrastructure and its replacement with other technologies needed to keep the site operating while the contamination was removed. John's management approach was collegial. In most organizations, those are just words. John walked the walk. His staff were his colleagues in every sense. He provided everything needed for success and held everyone accountable for that success. He led from behind (an overused phrase) by listening first, sometimes never saying anything for a long time, until we had sorted out our ideas ourselves. He allowed us to "think out loud," then act on those decisions with his support.

Two other managers have had that kind of influence on my growth as a program manager. Jack Pritchard was a vice president at Logicon where I managed a software development group. Jack always had sage advice for us young managers. He was the model of how to manage creative people while still getting the job done on-time, on-budget, and on-specification. Before Logicon, my first "manager" was Fred Leary, when I was a fresh graduate student writing radar signal processing code for the Air Force. I was locked away inside a literal vault, pouring over tens of thousands of lines of FORTRAN, so it was an encouragement when Fred came by to ask a simple question: "Is there anything I can do to improve what you are doing?" Usually, the answer was no, but when it was yes he went and did it and came back with the solution. He was an example of how to manage creative people—give them a clear, concise, definitive, and measurable task, provide all the needed resources, and let them do their job. He only intervened when he could actually add measurable value. No "supervision," no "oversight." Coaching, mentoring, and making small suggestions to keep everyone "inside the white lines" of the road we were on.

Over the course of writing this book, I have had a "day job." This involves managing projects and pieces of projects, advising those managing projects, and contributing to the policy-making side of defense program management through professional organizations and consulting engagements with the policy makers themselves in the Office of Secretary of Defense. Along the way I met many good project and program managers and a few that struggled for success. Each has provided insight into the Five Immutable Principles, Five Immutable Practices, and the processes you'll find in the book.

In the end, this book would not have happened without the support of my wife of twenty-five years, Linda Chartier. Linda understood that working two jobs, book and day job, meant sitting in the office long after everyone else was asleep, typing away. She not only tolerated it but also recognized the energy that comes from any difficult intellectual pursuit.

To all who have contributed to forming these ideas, I thank you. Some are credited directly and some may recognize your concepts. Newton's quote "I stand on the shoulders of giants" is appropriate, although the actual quote was a veiled insult to Hooke.[*] But my statement is meant as it is used today—"I could not have arrived here, without the knowledge and support of others."

---

[*] "Newton to Hooke," 5 Feb. 1676, in *The Correspondence of Isaac Newton*, edited by H. W. Turnbull, J. F. Scott, and A. R. Hall. 7 vols. (Cambridge: Cambridge University Press), I, 416, 1959.

INTRODUCTION

Project success is an elusive goal in every business or technical domain. Examples of project failure are easy to find. Examples of project success are not as well documented. We tend to focus on the failures rather than the successes. It is difficult to look for the root causes of project failure; instead, we tend to write about the magnitude of the failure and how things went wrong. Corrective actions are rarely discussed based on an assessment of the root causes, because the project participants have usually moved on. When we do look in greater detail, the literature shows the primary root causes of failure start with a failure to define what "done" looks like in any meaningful units of measure. Without a measurable assessment of progress toward "done," we cannot recognize "done" if or when we encounter it. In this book the word "done" has a special meaning. It means the customer is satisfied with the outcomes of the project. The customer must have specified these outcomes up front in the form of a set of capabilities the project will provide, with some unit of measure meaningful to the decision makers—the customer. This is a very specific definition and will be used throughout the book to mean "compliance with all the measures, technical and operational specifications, planned cost, and schedule."

Most practices, concepts, and language of project management we see today have their origins largely in the United States aerospace agencies in the mid-1950s. They were developed primarily for use on programs such as *Atlas, Polaris, Minuteman,* and *Apollo* manned space flight vehicles as a highly urgent response to the need to develop new ballistic missile capability to counter perceived Soviet threats. After that era, these processes were expanded through the U.S. Department of Defense (DoD) initiatives that capitalized on these practices and processes through today's methods.

Performance-Based Project Management[SM] is about successfully managing projects based on those early processes, but with the added concept of "capabilities," an idea derived from President John Kennedy's words of May 15, 1961: "To achieve the goal, before this decade is out, of landing a man on the moon and returning him safely to earth." This statement is the foundation of one of the Five Immutable Principles of project management: "Define what 'done' looks like in units of measure meaningful to the decision makers." Kennedy made this clear: fly to the moon, land, and return safely to earth. That statement defined success. That statement describes what "done" looks like. In the context of Kennedy's statement, a capability was the "ability" to fly to the moon, land, and return safely. For all projects, a set of "capability" statements is the starting point of describing "done."

My motivation for writing this book began decades ago when I moved from a career as a software developer on radar, sonar, and embedded control systems to focus on commercial software products. Clear and concise statements of effectiveness and performance guide the development of software and hardware for things that fly, drive, or swim away, and the control systems that manage them. When I moved to the commercial domain, those types of processes were frequently missing—not because the processes were not in place, but mainly because those asking for the projects were not aware of the fundamental need for defining what "done" looks like *before* starting the project. There were many books, journal papers, and articles describing the technical activities performed during the execution of the project. Many describe how to define strategic initiatives, business mission statements, and measures of performance for the business. But rarely did I encounter a source of guidance that connected the dots between a business strategy based on projects and the management of those projects. In the end, what was missing was a detailed description of how to connect business or mission strategy with project execution using the contents of this book.

Performance-Based Project Management is about the principles, practices, and processes of project management that make those connections. Before I begin showing you how to do this, I need to make a disclaimer. Although people execute these principles, practices, and processes, my focus in this book is not on people in a traditional manner. There are more than enough books about the "people" side of project management. People's processes change, and so does the underlying technology of managing a project. The team members, stakeholders, and the project managers looking after the project are probably not the same over the life of the project. People come and go. Technology comes and goes. What is "immutable" are the principles and the practices for how to successfully manage a project.

The singular beneficial takeaway of this book is:

> ➤ How to clearly define the purpose of the project; that is, how to have clarity of purpose,

> ➤ How to construct the artifacts, or elements, that represent that clarity, and

> ➤ How to measure the performance of the technical outcomes from the work on the project performed by the people.

Creating a clearly defined purpose starts with identifying the capabilities needed for business success. These capabilities are not just technical and operational requirements, they also are the "value" delivered by the project. However, this value must be measured in units meaningful to the consumer of the outcomes of the project. These are the Measures of Effectiveness (MoEs) for the artifacts and, thus, not just a statement of value, but the actual measures of that value.

Applying these principles, practices, and processes requires discipline. However, before we can have discipline, we need accountability. This accountability starts with making someone accountable for establishing, improving, and complying with the project management processes. These processes are based on practices, which, in turn, are based on principles. That is the message of this book: principles, practices, and processes are all needed for success.

The second aspect of accountability involves the roles and responsibilities assigned to each position on the project, by which I mean the project manager, team members, stakeholders, external resources, and senior management.

To create accountability, we have to convince all the participants in the project that they are actually "accountable" for the outcomes. This is often difficult, since each person involved in the project has to maintain accountability in order to move on to the next two steps—discipline and clarity of the outcome—for the project to succeed. When we fail to be clear about the outcome, the probability of success is reduced. For example, we might end up on time and on budget, but not produce the capabilities we need. Without discipline, it is difficult to apply the principles, practices, and processes, and without accountability, there is no mechanism for applying the discipline that is the basis for all we do in the project management domain.

After you read this book, I believe you will recognize that traditional approaches to managing a project need improvement. You'll start asking the question, "What does 'done' look like?" more often. You'll start asking the project owner questions about what capabilities are needed before you start developing requirements. Most of today's approaches to developing products or services start with the technical and operational requirements of the project. This leads to trouble later on when there is confusion about "why" those requirements are present.

Using the approach described in this book, you will be able to answer the five questions that form the basis of the Five Immutable Principles needed to increase the probability of a project's success:

1. What does "done" look like?

2. How are you going to reach "done"?

3. Do you have all the resources you need to reach "done"?

4. What impediments will you encounter along the way to "done"?

5. How are you going to measure progress toward "done" in units meaningful to the decision makers?

Once you know the answers to these questions, you can apply the Five Practices:

1. Define the needed capabilities.

2. Define the technical and operational requirements needed to implement those capabilities.

3. Establish a Performance Measurement Baseline (PMB) for performing the work that implements the requirements.

4. Execute the Performance Measurement Baseline.

5. Perform Continuous Risk Management (CRM) on everything you do on the project.

Once the principles and practices are in place, what remains are the Five Processes needed to manage the business activities of your project:

1. Organize the project with a work breakdown structure (WBS) and an organizational breakdown structure (OBS) to show what is being delivered and who is delivering it.

2. Plan, schedule, and budget the work needed to produce the deliverables.

3. Account for the time and money used to implement the deliverables.

4. Analyze the variances that result between the planned time and cost and the actual time and cost and measure the physical percent complete from those measures to determine actual progress to plan.

5. Maintain the integrity of all the information so forecasts of the project's future performance are based on a solid assessment of past performance.

These principles, practices, and processes are neither new nor unique. And they are not applied with any rigor outside the complex project management processes of government programs. What I have done in this book is distill the essence of the formal project management methods found in defense and space programs for application to a broader range of problems. All projects can be managed using the Performance-Based Project Management® method. No matter the size, complexity, or domain, the principles, practices, and processes can be applied to increase the probability of success.

Performance-Based Project Management is organized in a layered manner, starting with the principles. Before starting to apply the Five Immutable Principles I propose in this book, we should stop and re-member H. L. Mencken's advice: "For every complex problem, there is an answer that is clear, simple, and wrong." We need a set of principles on which to build our practices and processes.

Those readers who have looked at the contents page know that we don't jump right into the principles. Instead, in order to ground you, we start with the "drivers" of project success—the mechanics of how projects work. This will help you understand the data of the project, how the data interact, how the managers of the project can use data to make decisions, and how the data influence how these decisions are made.

Once the drivers of project success are in place, answers to the questions asked by the Five Principles can be developed, and, with these answers, we have what we need to confirm that the customer understands:

- ➤ What "done" looks like
- ➤ How we are going to get there
- ➤ What it is going to cost and how long it will take
- ➤ How we're going to handle all the impediments along the way
- ➤ Most important, how we are going to measure all these things to confirm we are actually making progress, not just spending money and passing the time

With the principles in place, we move on to how to do the following:

- ➤ Develop a description of the needed capabilities to be produced by the project.
- ➤ Develop the technical and operational requirements that pro-duce those capabilities.

> ➤ Plan the work needed to deliver those requirements.

> ➤ Perform that work.

> ➤ Manage all the risks that result from normal project work.

These practices are connected to the principles through step-by-step processes. The result is a description of what value is being delivered to the customer—the needed capabilities—and how that value is being delivered—both when and for how much. This approach provides actionable information to the decision makers so they can direct not only the work but also the beneficial outcomes.

The final step is to apply Five Processes to manage the underlying activities of the project. We have to know what we are building; who is actually doing the work to build the desired outcomes; the plans, schedule, and budgets needed to produce this work; and the data needed to show the project is actually on plan. These processes are the foundation on which the practices to implement the principles are performed.

With the principles, practices, and processes in place, we need to know how to tailor them to our own projects. Three projects—a personal Unmanned Aerial Vehicle (UAV), a kitchen remodel, and a health insurance provider network Enterprise Resource Planning (ERP) system—are described to demonstrate how the three elements of successful project management are applied. After an overview showing how to tailor the practices and processes, the details of how to implement them are provided so you can put the practices and processes to use on your own projects.

It is important to note that applying the practices and processes, tailored to your own project, results in a set of artifacts that are needed to actually manage the work. This is the final step in changing how projects are managed—moving project management from simply implementing technical and operational requirements to providing the needed capabilities that produce measurable business value to the customer.

With these principles, practices, and processes in place, you are ready to start increasing the probability of your project's success. For additional information about specific aspects of project management and details not covered here, consult the bibliography for additional source material.

CHAPTER 1

The Ten Drivers
of Project Success

Project success is elusive. Many books, articles, and professional socie-ties suggest methods that can be used to produce this success, and I be-lieve that anything and everything we read, listen to, and participate in around the notion of managing projects can add value to and increase the probability of a project's success.

Of course, anyone who has been around project management has anecdotes about failed projects and has participated in failed projects despite using the checklists, flowcharts, tools, competency assessments, and certifications designed to improve the chances of producing a suc-cessful project. In each of these cases, the project failed because some-thing was missing.

To optimize project success, we need to look to the foundation of all project success, the immutable principles and practices of managing projects.

The Five Immutable Principles of project management success are built on ten success drivers, which are the underlying mechanics of all project work. They are the core processes that take place during the life of any project (see Figure 1.1). The *Five Practices* used during the management of projects are built on the *Five Immutable Principles*. The relationship between the principles and the practices is important to the success of any project. Without first establishing the principles, the practices have no foundation on which to "practice." Figure 1.2 shows how these drivers relate to one another. We'll look at them in detail later in the chapter. The principles, which are built on the drivers, and the practices, which are built on the principles, are the foundation of project success. This does not mean success is assured, but it does mean that without them the project has less of a chance of success.

The success drivers are organized into three classes:

1. **Planning.** We need a plan, a schedule, a budget, a description of the work to be performed, and the order in which that work should be performed.

2. **Execution.** Once the work is defined and the required order established, execution of the work packages (WPs) can take place.

3. **Performance Management.** While the work is being performed, we need to measure our progress against the plan. This measurement should be tangible, not just an opinion. The best tangible evidence is confirmation that the planned outcome of each work package actually occurred at the planned time for the planned budget.

Figure 1.1 summarizes the principles, practices, and drivers and their functions. As we proceed with this chapter, we will explore each in greater detail.

Project success depends on doing many things right, each of which must operate as a close-knit system, supporting each other in order to deliver a successful project. It all begins with the drivers of the Five

FIGURE 1.1 The foundation of project success starts with the ten drivers.

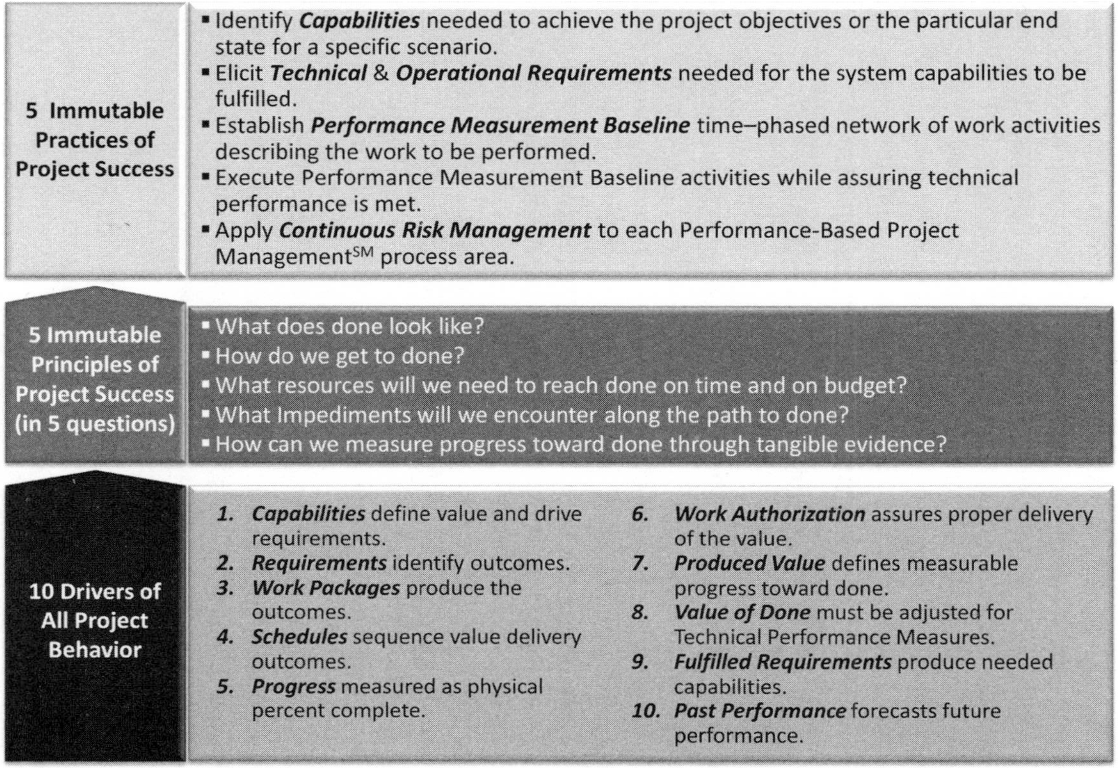

5 Immutable Practices of Project Success

- Identify *Capabilities* needed to achieve the project objectives or the particular end state for a specific scenario.
- Elicit *Technical & Operational Requirements* needed for the system capabilities to be fulfilled.
- Establish *Performance Measurement Baseline* time–phased network of work activities describing the work to be performed.
- Execute Performance Measurement Baseline activities while assuring technical performance is met.
- Apply *Continuous Risk Management* to each Performance-Based Project Management^SM process area.

5 Immutable Principles of Project Success (in 5 questions)

- What does done look like?
- How do we get to done?
- What resources will we need to reach done on time and on budget?
- What Impediments will we encounter along the path to done?
- How can we measure progress toward done through tangible evidence?

10 Drivers of All Project Behavior

1. *Capabilities* define value and drive requirements.
2. *Requirements* identify outcomes.
3. *Work Packages* produce the outcomes.
4. *Schedules* sequence value delivery outcomes.
5. *Progress* measured as physical percent complete.
6. *Work Authorization* assures proper delivery of the value.
7. *Produced Value* defines measurable progress toward done.
8. *Value of Done* must be adjusted for Technical Performance Measures.
9. *Fulfilled Requirements* produce needed capabilities.
10. *Past Performance* forecasts future performance.

Immutable Principles of project management and the Five Practices that implement these principles. They and their relationship to one another are illustrated in Figure 1.2. Without understanding the drivers, there is no real way to check the validity of the principles or practices. These drivers are found in any project, in any business, in any technical domain, using any project management or product development method.

The Immutable Principles and Practices of Project Success

There is an unspoken question in the project management community: *How can we integrate strategic, technical, and managerial processes into a framework based on sound principles, while providing practices that can be applied in a wide variety of domains?*

There are numerous approaches to managing projects. Many can be found in books like *A Guide to the Project Management Body of Knowledge* (*PMBOK® Guide*), in Prince2®, and in agile software development books. These describe the technical and operational side of project management. The management of cost, schedule, and technical performance can be extracted from these descriptions. Human actions relevant to the management of projects—such as communications, the intent of the leaders, understanding, uncertainty, and the tacit knowledge required to successfully deliver the project's value to the stakeholders—are also taken into account in these descriptions. A recurring theme in all these methods is that *good project management practices need to be built on principles.* "Best practices" alone are necessary, but they are not sufficient. Practices, even ones built on sound principles, must be effective in the face of uncertainty, confusion, and ever-present change. With this in mind, we need to search for the drivers that are the foundation of the Five Principles. The Five Practices are then built on these Five Principles. These drivers are the source of both project difficulties and project success. When the driver is absent, the project is missing information needed for success. When the driver is present, it is connected

FIGURE 1.2 How the ten drivers relate to one another.

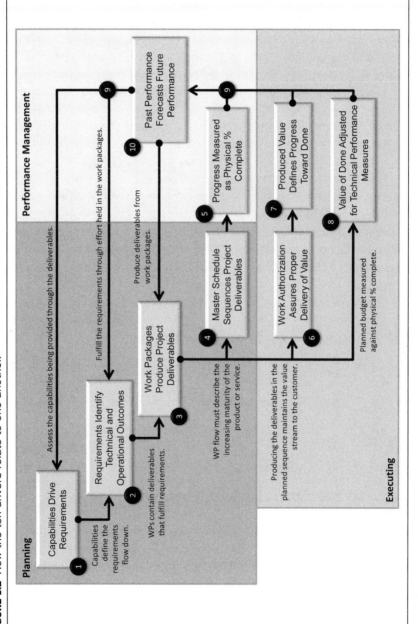

to a principle, which in turn is connected to a practice to increase the probability of success. Without understanding of what "drives" success or failure, the project manager has no insight into how to manage the project to produce success. The project manager is unable to "connect the dots" between what is happening in the project and what *should be* happening to increase the probability of the project's success.

Traditionally, a set of project management activities (e.g., product or service integration, cost, communication, scope, quality, risk, time, human resources, and procurement) is applied throughout the management of the project. These activities focus on the *execution* of the project.

This approach has shortcomings in our quest to increase the probability of project success. For example, the previous list of project activities does not include project strategy, creation of value from the project, measurement of effectiveness of the resulting outcomes, or measures of performance of the work activities in units meaningful to the decision makers.

The Basis of the Five Immutable Principles

Some people in the field talk about the "basic tenets" of project management. But where do these come from? Some say they come from hands-on experience, anecdotal "best practices," and the good old "school of hard knocks."

According to *Webster's Dictionary*, a *principle* is a "general truth, a law on which other laws are founded or from which others are derived." In the project management domain, a principle can be further defined as:[1]

> ➤ A rule or law of action based on desirable ends or objectives based on a fundamental set of actions. Principles are the basis of policies or procedures that govern the behavior of the people, processes, and tools used on a project. One common principle is, "time is money." In all project work this is the case. If work is being done, time is passing, and people must be paid for their time.

> ➤ A fundamental truth that can explain the relationship between project variables—usually cost, time, or technical attributes.

These can be independent and dependent variables in this relationship. This fundamental truth can be descriptive, explaining what will happen, or it can be prescriptive, indicating what a person, a process, or a tool should do based on some known standard. The principle can also reflect a scale of values, such as efficiency, reliability, availability, or other "...ilities." In this case, ... *ilities* imply value judgments as well as actual measurements. In another example, cost and schedule are directly related through some multiplicative factor. The more time the project takes, assuming constant productivity of the labor, the larger the cost will be for that labor. Quality, cost, and schedule performance can be described in the same way, with the same productivity factors. Technical performance of the planned deliverables is also related to cost and schedule in the same way.

For the principles of project management to be effective, Max Wideman suggests they must do the following:[2]

> "Express a general or fundamental truth, a basic concept...

> "Make for a high probability of project success. The corollary is that the absence of the condition will render project success on a majority of the key criteria as being highly improbable.

> "Provide the basis for establishing logical processes and supporting practices that can be proven through research, analysis, and practical testing...

> "Be universal to all areas of project management application.

> "Be capable of straightforward expression in one or two sentences.

> "Be self-evident to experienced project management personnel, and

> "Carry a concise label reflecting its content."

Max Wideman's PM Glossary (www.maxwideman.com) is a great source of information about project management terminology.

The Five Principles

The Five Immutable Principles of Performance-Based Project Management are designed to meet both the definitions of a principle and Wideman's requirement that they be effective. Here, they are stated as questions that need to be answered by the project manager:

1. Where are we going?
2. How are we going to get there?
3. Do we have everything we need?
4. What impediments will we encounter, and how will we remove them?
5. How are we going to measure our progress?

These questions can be applied to projects just as they can be applied to any endeavor from flying to Mars to taking a family vacation. If we use the dictionary definition of *immutable,* "not subject or susceptible to change or variation in form or quality or nature," we can apply these principles to any project in any business or technical domain.

The Five Practices

The Five Practices, which are derived from the Five Immutable Principles, are used to keep the project on track:

1. Identify needed capabilities.
2. Define a requirements baseline.
3. Develop a Performance Measurement Baseline.
4. Execute the Performance Measurement Baseline.
5. Apply Continuous Risk Management.

The Ten Drivers of the Principles That Enable the Practices

Let's look at the ten drivers shown in Figure 1.2 that are the foundation for the immutable principles and practices of project success.

1. **Capabilities drive system requirements.** Capabilities provide the customer with the means to generate business or mission value. With these capabilities in hand, the mission or business need can be carried out and the desired beneficial outcome produced from the project. If we understand what capabilities are needed to produce business value or satisfy a mission, we can then identify what technical or operation requirements are needed to deliver those capabilities.

2. **Requirements are defined in work packages.** Requirements are derived from the needed capabilities by asking and answering the question, "How can this capability be delivered using the technical or operational solutions at hand?" The mechanisms for implementing a capability are described in a requirement. Requirements state the "shalls" of the solution in support of a capability. The requirements are implemented in work packages (WPs), which produce deliverables that are assembled into the capability that produces the products or services needed by the customer.

3. **Work packages produce the deliverables.** This is where labor and materials come together; it is where the work needed to produce the components of products or services is done.

4. **The Performance Measurement Baseline (PMB) describes the work sequence.** The PMB is the time-phased arrangement of the work packages that produce usable results in a planned order to produce the desired product or service.

5. **Measures of physical percent complete define "done" for each work package.** Working software, usable products or services, all measured in predefined units of "physical percent complete," provide the evidence needed to demonstrate that work is progressing according to plan.

6. **Work authorization assures proper delivery of value.** Keeping the work flowing to maximize the delivered product or service requires a well-structured schedule.

7. **Produced and measurable value defines progress.** Measurement in units of effectiveness and performance for the user is the definition of value that all projects require.

8. **All measures are adjusted for technical performance compliance.** Performance to plan is adjusted for the technical and operational aspects of the project, not just the passage of time and consumption of resources. These adjustments are necessary to correct our measures of effectiveness of our cost and schedule. If we planned to complete a deliverable in a specific amount of time for a specific amount of money and that deliverable was not technically compliant, we would have to spend more money and time to finish it. Therefore, we would be over budget and late on the planned day of completion of our deliverable.

9. **Fulfilled requirements produce delivered capabilities.** With the requirement fulfilled by products or services, the capabilities can be deployed to the customer.

10. **Past performance is a forecast of future performance.** For all measurements of future performance, what happened before is a good starting point.

The ten "driving" elements shown in Figure 1.2 illustrate the various activities applied across the life cycle of a project or program. They start at the inception of the project (Driver 1) and the initial assessment of the business's or system's capabilities and continue through requirements elicitation (Driver 2) and the creation of the PMB describing the time phased work and its budget (Driver 3 and 4), to the execution of the baseline (Drivers 6, 7, and 8) and project close-out (Drivers 9 and 10).

The drivers of Performance-Based Project Management provide feedback loops to assure that subsequent activities provide measurable information about the corrective actions needed to increase the probability of success. This repeated step-by-step approach to project management assures that the periods of assessment provided for corrective actions are appropriately spaced to minimize risk and maximize the delivered value to the project.

The ten drivers are the basis of the principles and practices of Performance-Based Project Management, and each is present in every project domain, every business paradigm, and in every project management method. If the driver is not recognized and dealt with, it will still "drive" the project outcome, whether the project manager looks after its performance or not. For example, if the work is performed out of sequence, the project is missing Driver 6: Work Authorization, and the work products may need rework. If we install the wallboard in the house before the electrical wiring, we will have to cut the wallboard to pull the wiring.

Putting the Ten Drivers to Work

Let's look in more detail at each driver and see how addressing it with the Five Immutable Principles and Five Practices can increase the probability of project success.

Capabilities Drive System Requirements

The first driver of project success is the principle that all technical and operational requirements must be derived from the needed capabilities.

We hear all the time about bloated software products, with features no one uses. But what we don't hear about is how to address this supposed issue. It turns out all the capabilities in those products are needed by someone—maybe not us, but someone. They are there for a purpose. Maybe not the right purpose, but they didn't get there by accident. Knowing up front what capabilities are needed for a product is not an accident, either. This is the role of *capabilities-based planning*. What capabilities do we need for the project to be successful?

Defining a capability creates the flexibility needed to ensure system responsiveness and sustainability in the presence of constant change.[3]

At the same time, we need to deliver tangible benefits to the user. These capabilities may include:

> **Agility.** Adapting to emerging situations that had not been planned for or even foreseen.

> **Tailorability.** Changing the behavior of the product or service to meet emerging needs.

> **Architecture.** Measuring the coupling and cohesion (interrelationships) between the business processes that support agility and tailorability with the least amount of disruption to previously developed project outcomes.[4]

Project governance provides the guidance needed to institutionalize a capabilities-based approach. Project governance requires continued assessment and evolution in support of the tangible benefits:

> Enforcement of rules and responsibilities on the organization and its members

> Guidance of the flow of work to sustain the needed performance of the business or mission

> Continuous improvement of the people, processes, and tools

> Facilitation of transformation from the current state to some desired future state

The core concept of capabilities-based planning is its focus on the delivery of business or mission value, or "value-focused thinking," which, in turn, is based on two methods for making decisions: the first focuses on competitive analysis of the various alternatives, and the second on attaining organizational values as the fundamental objective of any decision-making process.[5]

In order to describe each capability, assumptions must be made without any specific technical and operational information. To avoid unwelcome surprises, some form of assumptions-based planning is needed. This requires taking five actions:

1. Make operational plans about how we are going to use the capabilities that result from the project ("What would we do

with the products or services if they showed up tomorrow and were free?").

2. Describe plausible events—that is, the things we know have a chance of happening.

3. Identify the signposts for potential problems that can then be used to monitor the things that can go wrong with our project.

4. Discover shaping actions that shore up uncertain assumptions about the future. We can't control the weather, but we can control whether we are going to eat outside or stay in.

5. Take hedging actions to better prepare for the possibility that an assumption will fail by thinking through plausible scenarios to test the assumptions. This *what-if* approach is at the core of good project risk management.[6]

Capabilities-based planning makes use of these assumption-development processes to describe system capabilities when there are no specific technical or operational requirements. These development processes allow project managers to do the following:

> ➤ Discover what is not known by reaching a sufficient basic level of knowledge of the parameters of the problem.

> ➤ Identify problems by understanding the current process, along with the people and technology involved.

The next step establishes boundaries and the elements of the solution. These are grouped into three types of principles:

1. **Orientation** principles align the development process on a sound theoretical basis using generally accepted practices in the areas of engineering, modeling, and acquisition. These principles include: Capability Thinking, Architecture Models, Evolutionary Development, and Deliverables-Centric Planning. When we think of capabilities, we can ask, "What do I need to get the job done?" "I need to process transactions for $0.07 each, rather than the current $0.11." When thinking about architecture, an external framework is the starting point. "We must

be SOA compliant for this project to be successful." Evolutionary development establishes the sequence of capabilities to be delivered over time. "Enroll all members using the new system and process them using the legacy system. With them all enrolled, we can then migrate to the second phase of using a third–party processing system." Deliverables-centric orientation is the basis of all project success. The customer bought the deliverable, not the work efforts—actually, not even the technology. The customer bought the ability to "do something."

2. **Communication** principles enforce the standardization of vocabulary and structure of information to be exchanged within or outside the system. These include standardized formats and common terminology to describe the system capabilities. The semantics used to describe what "done" looks like need to be shared between the provider and the consumer. Without this commonality, it will be difficult to determine if the needed capabilities have actually been provided at the end of the project.

3. **Collaboration** principles enable active and timely participation of all stakeholders involved in the production of a capability. These include collaborative engineering and information sharing between the contributors of the system capability elements. Development of solution is a collaborative effort guided by the shared understanding of what "done" looks like. There must be information exchanged between the provider and the consumer to ensure that each is using the same units of measure. An Interface Control Document (ICO) is an example of this shared understanding. It states the protocols and format of data, processes, and outcomes on both sides of the interface.

Requirements Identify Technical and Operational Outcomes

Inadequate requirements engineering is a common problem in the development of any complex system.[7] A "requirement" is an attribute of the resulting product or service. It is a statement of a capability or a quality needed to provide value to the buyer. Without proper requirements, neither the provider nor the customer can know what "done" looks like in any meaningful way. The result is confusion, rework, missing features, or less-than-acceptable outcomes. Although there are many resources that explain how to capture requirements, each requirement needs a *home,* a reason for existing. When a requirement is fulfilled, the outcome is a *capability,* which means the users can now do something with it. They can put it to work.

There are many issues associated with requirements engineering, including failure to define the scope of the system in terms of capabilities. Failure to foster understanding among the communities affected by the development of a given system often starts because the needs for these requirements are missing or not fully explained. These are elicitation issues. They occur before the requirements engineering process starts and are at the heart of poor systems requirements. The industry average investment in a requirements process is 2 to 3 percent of the total project cost.[8] This investment is trivial compared to the risk of delivering a less than acceptable outcome from the project. The classic example is the enterprise IT project, where the users don't actually know what they want the system to do. Instead, they have the developers start producing software, hoping to discover the final outcomes as they proceed. With a small investment for the total project, clarity can be produced to guide the development effort. We would never start building a custom kitchen remodel without some understanding of what "done" looks like.

This problem leads to the creation of poor requirements and burdens the development process. The system developed will later be judged unsatisfactory or unacceptable, as a result of high maintenance costs and frequent changes.[9] By improving the process by which requirements are obtained, the requirements engineering process can be improved, resulting in enhanced system requirements and potentially a much better system.

After requirements elicitation, requirements engineering is deconstructed into the activities of requirements elicitation, specification, and validation. Most of today's requirements techniques and tools focus on specification (i.e., the way in which the requirements are described). The Five Principles and Practices of the Performance-Based

Project Management approach concentrate on elicitation concerns, those problems with requirements engineering that are not adequately addressed by specification techniques. Cristel provides one elicitation methodology to handle these concerns: A conversation takes place between designers, customers, and implementers in which they pool their perspective expertise and viewpoints to resolve design issues.[10] The details of this approach will be developed in Chapter 3.

When we get to Chapter 3's requirements process, we will use these universal process steps:[11]

1. **Elicitation.** Identify who the sources of information about the system are, and find out the requirements from them.

2. **Analysis.** Understand the requirements; look for where they overlap and where areas of conflict might exist.

3. **Validation.** Go back to the system stakeholders to determine if the requirements really do meet their needs.

4. **Negotiation.** Inevitably, stakeholders' views will differ, and proposed requirements might conflict. Try to reconcile conflicting views and generate a consistent set of requirements.

5. **Documentation.** Write the requirements in a way that stakeholders and product developers can understand them.

6. **Management.** Control the inevitable changes to the requirements changes through a formal change control process, documenting the baseline requirements and all changes to this baseline.

Work Packages Produce Project Deliverables

Project success requires staying focused on separating the various system capabilities into clearly defined streams based on their function defined by the requirements elicitation process. This effort decouples the technical functionality from the system capabilities, increasing cohesion and reducing coupling between each stream.

This deconstruction process is almost never optimal the first time around. The false sense of urgency to deconstruct the system requirements into a work breakdown structure (WBS) will cause extra work later on.

Investing in a carefully developed WBS will pay back later in the project by isolating the work processes into supporting value streams.

In the world of agile software development, the WBS may appear to be an odd artifact. In fact, agile methods employ WBSs as well. They are called storyboards, use cases, and other organizing paradigms. The key to all project success is to know the structure of the delivered capabilities, how the components of these capabilities interact with each other, and what the dependencies and the hierarchy of the components are. Without some form of product and service deconstruction, it is difficult to know what "done" looks like.

There is no set of instructions for how to do this. But starting the WBS in a graphical form, putting that diagram on the wall, and asking the coupling and cohesion questions about the terminal nodes in the WBS is one way. (An example of the terminal nodes can be found in Figure 4.3.) This "sticky notes on the wall" approach is found in many other project management processes, not just Agile.

The construction of the WBS and the resulting work packages starts with breaking down the requirements into collections of deliverables. Focusing on the deliverables is critical for the following reasons:

> All resources—internal and external, their dependents, and any other items needed to produce the deliverables—are defined in the work packages. The work package manager is accountable for managing all of these resources.

> The work packages that result from this deconstruction are the vehicles for producing the deliverables.

> When these deliverables exist, they provide the capabilities the system needs to perform its function.

If resources are not controlled by the work package manager, the risk to the success of the deliverables is greatly increased:

> Accountability is no longer traceable to a single person, violating the principles of the Responsibility Assignment Matrix (RAM) (as shown in Figure 4.3).

> Performance reporting for physical percent complete is no longer represented by tangible items within the work package.

Each work package produces one deliverable. This deliverable may have a Technical Performance Measure (TPM) attached—a Measure of Performance (MoP) or Measure of Effectiveness (MoE). Measures of Performance characterize the physical and functional attributes relating to the operation of the system operation, measured or estimated under specific testing and/or operational environmental conditions. MoEs are operational measures closely related to the achievement of the mission or operational objective being evaluated, in its intended operational environment under a specified set of conditions. MoEs state how well the system achieves its intended purpose. The Technical Performance Measures connect the dots between cost, schedule, and the technical maturity of the deliverable.[12]

In the absence of Technical Performance Measures, the Performance Measurement Baseline lacks the ability to connect the physical percent complete with the increasing maturity of the product or service.

The Master Schedule Sequences the Outcomes of Work Packages

Arranging the work packages in a logical network is an iterative process. It should be obvious which major deliverables come first, second, and so on. Building an initial network, plotting that network on a big visible chart,[13] hanging that chart on the wall, and standing in front of it with all the work package managers is part of developing a credible plan for the project.

The plan is the strategy for delivering the business capabilities the customer asked for. With a big visible chart, the strategy is able to be seen—or at least is more easily seen—than a list of work packages would be.[14] The strategy for delivering the project can be mapped out in a *wall-walk* manner to make the connections obvious. The wall-walk is a process where sticky notes or any type of temporary documents are placed on a wall and participants "walk" these notes and talk about their contents and how that content describes the outcomes of the project. The project members then try to convince the other members that they have the needed information to start their work. This hands-on approach is much better than burying the descriptions of the project's outcome in a project plan or spreadsheet. This process ensures that each project member has a clear and concise description of what he or she is to produce and what is to be received from the other members. This agreement on the exchange of information and the exchange of artifacts ensures that the proper order of work is established. (Chapter 4 will provide more detail on planning, scheduling, and budgeting this work.)

Creating the first cut of a credible plan and its schedule using the work packages is a *hands-on* process. It starts with six simple rules:

1. All relationships between WPs are "finish to start." This initial arrangement provides visibility into which parts of the work are dependent on other parts of the work being completed. This, in turn, drives schedule compression. Non–finish-to-start relationships lead to partially complete work being used in future efforts, which results in "rework," because the earlier work was incomplete.

2. There should be no "lead" or "lag" arrangements between WPs. These create hidden dependencies and hidden schedule compression, and produce partially complete work products for consumption that need to be updated when the work package is completed.

3. The only constraints on the network should be a *must start on* (MSO) for the start date and an *as soon as possible* (ASAP) for all other activities. Any other constraints create hidden dependencies. This may appear hard to do, but it is the basis for an "ideal" schedule. Other constraints may be added later, but only for necessary reasons to control the flow of work in the schedule. External dependencies are the primary reasons for these constraints. The arrival of material or waiting for the completion of an external activity are simple examples.

4. The flow of WPs should create a description of the increasing maturity of the products or services produced by the project, not just an account of which resources were consumed and what deliverables were produced. The description of maturity should be meaningful to the customer in terms of business capabilities or mission fulfillment attributes resulting from the completion

of each WP. This maturity is measured by the ability to perform a capability. Throughput of a process can be a measure of maturity. The "preliminary" capability is for small batches of recycling containers from the neighborhood trash collection service. The final capability can be for the full-rate production of the batch processing of the entire city's trash. As the processing plant "matures," the process details can be worked out.

5. Describing the plan and schedule in these terms gives the customer insight into the actual progress of the project. Describing them in terms of consumption of resources, production of products, or passage of milestones is not meaningful to the customer.

6. Single point estimates of cost and schedule are meaningless without providing the range of values, the level of confidence in achieving each value, and an analysis of how these estimates will impact the credibility of the project being completed on time, on schedule, and with the planned technical performance.

These rules appear very detailed, but, in fact, they are only a hint of how detailed a project manager must be to produce a credible, ultimately successful, plan and schedule, and they are critical success factors for all projects. They must be addressed up front and throughout the project. The project manager must understand all the dependencies between work activities and must be able to foresee conflicts, roadblocks, and risks if there is any chance of completing on time and on budget.

Work Package Progress Measured as Physical Percent Complete

Measures of "progress to plan" can only be done with measures that describe tangible evidence of progress. Any other measure of progress cannot be connected to the delivery of business value to the customer. This is the basis of earned value, management agile software development methodologies, and the principles of capabilities-based planning.

At the work activity level, using the 0 percent/100 percent assessment is the best approach. Either we are done or we are not done. It's as simple as that. When these work activities are collected in a work package, we can now measure the physical percent complete by summing the completeness of the work activities for that WP. The cumulative value of the physical percent complete of each activity is the indicator of how much progress is being made.

There is no need to ask people where they are in their plan. Simply ask, "What work have we accomplished against our planned work as of the status date?" In other words, "Did we do what we planned to do by a given date?" If not, then, "When will we actually do it?" It is the old cliché, "Plan the work and work the plan." It might sound trite, but it is a critical success factor in any project management method.

There are eight simple steps for measuring progress to plan, using physical percent complete:

1. Use each work activity in the WP to provide some form of progress toward producing the deliverable.

2. Use this progress as an incremental measure of the overall progress of the WP.

3. Predefine how each work effort contributes to the overall progress of the WP.

4. Have the owner of the WP describe the incremental physical percent complete in terms of tangible evidence of progress to plan.

5. Ensure that what "done" looks like is defined in terms of the physical percent complete of the work package, Measures of Effectiveness (MoE), and Measures of Performance (MoP).

6. Capture this definition in the WP documentation.

7. Ask this question: *How long are we willing to wait before we find out we are late?*

8. Measure physical progress to plan before that period of performance arrives, leaving enough lead time so management corrections can be made to stay on cost and schedule, and meet technical performance requirements.

Work Authorization Assures Delivery as Planned

A work authorization system assures that the proper sequence of work is conveyed to those performing the work. We would not want to install the furniture before we installed the carpet in our new home. The same is true of software projects, building projects, or training projects. There is a natural sequence for doing the work that provides a logical progression and produces value for the project.

It is important for project managers to be aware of how they convey the work authorization to their staff. To ensure that spoken words are not misinterpreted, written directions provide this explicit guidance for each work package.

The work package can be anything that might need to be accomplished to produce a deliverable. By providing a written work authorization, those in project management can be assured that their wish to have the job done by the right people, at the correct time, and in the right order can be executed.

The project manager needs to be cautious when writing out the exact steps on the work authorization to prevent misunderstandings and mistakes along the line. For the work to be done correctly the first time, the manager must be able to communicate well. This applies to both the writing of the authorization and the oral answers to any questions that might arise. Proper direction given to staff in the work-authorization directive will ensure that the task is completed in the expected manner.

Controlling the sequence of work has measurable benefits for the project:

> ➤ Executing the work packages in the agreed sequence ensures that the project will proceed as planned.

>> • This approach starts with a work authorization and control processes and requires the continual monitoring of late starts, late finishes, schedule margin erosion, and TPM compliance.

>> • The work authorization ensures that work is performed in the planned sequence, employing the planned programmatic risk reduction, to continuously increase the maturity of the product or service.

> ➤ "Out of sequence work" creates programmatic and technical risks.

- It disrupts the measures of physical percent complete—work without a plan and a plan without the work hide project performance.

- It disrupts the strategy developed for sequencing work to increase the maturity of the product or service.

Produced Value Defines Project Progress

Measuring the consumption of budget against the production of value is the role of any Performance-Based Project Management system. In Chapter 5, the concept of Earned Value Management (EVM) is examined in more detail.

For now, it is important to know that there are seven principles of EVM that are applicable to all project performance measurement:

1. Plan the scope of all the work required for the project from inception to completion. This doesn't mean "plan at the detailed level." It means "have a plan," know what capabilities are needed, and have a notion of how to deliver them.

2. Break down the project work scope into finite pieces that can be assigned to a responsible person or organization for control of technical, schedule, and cost objectives.

3. Integrate project work scope, schedule, and cost objectives into a Performance Measurement Baseline plan against which accomplishments may be measured. Control changes to this baseline.

4. Use actual costs incurred and recorded in accomplishing the work performed.

5. Objectively assess—using tangible evidence of physical percent complete—accomplishments at the work performance level.

6. Analyze significant variances from the plan and how these affect forecasts, and prepare an estimate of completion based on performance to date and work to be performed.

7. Use this performance information in the organization's management processes.

Adjust Value with Technical Performance Measures

Technical Performance Measures are defined and evaluated to assess how well a system is achieving its performance requirements. A TPM tells us what the product or service should be doing when it is working correctly. It can be an attribute of the product—size, weight, speed, reliability—or it can be a measure of the business value—reduced cost, improved throughput, increased profit margin.

Typically, dozens of TPMs are defined for a system. Yet, although they generate useful information and data about a system's performance, little is available in the project management community on how to integrate these measures into a meaningful assessment of the system's overall technical and programmatic performance risk. The TPMs are connected to the deliverables from the project. The programmatic performance assesses the effectiveness of cost and schedule in producing those deliverables.

TPMs can be combined to measure and monitor the overall performance risk of a system by integrating individual TPMs in a way that produces an overall risk index.

The project manager must be cognizant of three basic project risk elements (baselines):

1. Cost
2. Schedule
3. Technical performance

Cost and schedule are tracked through cost and schedule control systems (earned value). Technical performance is tracked using the TPM system, which is the project manager's early warning system when correlated to cost and schedule reports to provide the complete status of the project.

The TPM method selects technical performance parameters, assigning weights, linking to WBS, planning progress over time, getting data, evaluating variances, and taking corrective action as needed. Variances indicate the level of risk and detect new risks before their effects on cost/schedule are irrevocable.

The TPM approach involves:

> Assessing technical characteristics of the system and identifying problems through tests/analyses

> Surfacing inadequacies in time and dollars

> Matching cost against schedule performance

> Providing a basis for cost/schedule revisions

> Facilitating the verification of results achieved against technical requirements and what remaining technical work can be accomplished within established budgets

Performance Feedback Adjusts Schedule and Resource Allocation

Project management performance measurements must integrate cost and schedule parameters with the assessment of technical outcomes in order to assess the future performance of the project and act as an early warning system in the event something is going wrong.

As far back as 1997, the discussion centered on integrating cost, schedule, and technical performance. Robust project performance management processes must provide technical performance measures and exit criteria for assessing technical maturity that are quantitatively linked to measures of cost and schedule.

These measures of TPM compliance adjust our measures of future performance and our estimates of the final cost and completion dates when there is less-than-planned-for technical performance, such as poor quality, missing scope, delayed scope, or combinations of these.

These TPMs tell us how well a system is achieving its performance requirements. Technical Performance Measurement uses actual or predicted values from engineering measurements, tests, experiments, or prototypes.

To provide feedback for adjusting the forecasted cost and schedule we need to:

> Include systems engineering activities in the schedule and the Performance Measurement Baseline (PMB)

> ➤ Establish thresholds or parameters for TPM in the project plan

> ➤ Specify objective measures of progress as base measures for EVM for development maturity to date, product's ability to satisfy requirements, and product metrics, including TPM achievement to date

> ➤ Review the project's plans, activities, work products, and PMB for consistency with the requirements and the changes made to the requirements baseline

> ➤ Incorporate risk mitigation plans in the project plan, including changes to the PMB

> ➤ Include quantified risk assessments in the estimate at completion (EAC), depending on the probability of risk occurrence and the impact on cost objectives

Past Performance Forecasts Future Performance

Employing measures of cost, schedule, and technical performance provides the project manager with data needed to take corrective actions. Learn from the past to correct the future. This is a critical role of the project manager. Two metrics are particularly useful in the management of any project, program, or portfolio of projects.[15]

The Cost Performance Index (CPI) is a reflection of a project's cost efficiency. The CPI tells us how much physical work was accomplished, expressed as the budgeted value, against how much actual cost has been incurred to accomplish the performed work.

The question: *Is the project staying on target, underrunning, or perhaps overrunning costs?*

Perfect cost performance would be defined as CPI = 1.0: For every dollar we spend, we get an outcome worth one dollar. Sometimes we do better, sometimes worse. The CPI is an indicator of past cost performance. The second metric, To Complete Performance Index (TCPI), focuses on future performance.

The question: *What will it take to meet the goals set by management?* The TCPI works in conjunction with the CPI:

TCPI = Cost of the work remaining / Funds remaining

Looking Back

The ten drivers of project success form the basis of the Five Immutable Principles of project management and can be applied to every project in every business and technical domain.

They will be developed in detail in the coming chapters, but it is worth a quick review here, before moving on:

1. Do we know what "done" looks like?

2. Do we know how we are going to reach "done"?

3. Do we have all the resources needed to reach "done"?

4. What impediments are we going to encounter along the way and how are we going to handle them?

5. How are we going to measure progress in units of measure meaningful to the decision makers?

These Five Immutable Principles are applicable to every project in every business and technical domain. That is the definition of *immutable*—they never change and are universally applicable.

What's Ahead?

In the coming chapters, we'll examine how each of the Five Principles guides the application of the practices needed for project success and how each principle depends on the other four. We'll also explore the five work processes needed to provide information to make decisions about the progress of any project.

These Five Immutable Principles, their practices, and the work processes will then be assembled into a Project Management Method, which, when applied, increases the probability of a project's success. This is the result of simple attributes of Performance-Based Project Management that are not found in any other approach to managing projects:

> A plan is defined that shows what capabilities are needed at what point in the project life cycle to produce continuous delivery of business value to the stakeholders. This plan shows:

  • The "value flow" of delivered capabilities

  • The evaluation points to ensure progress is being made as planned in the delivery of this value

> Work is performed in the proper sequence to ensure that this value is actually delivered.

  • The capacity for work and the sequence of that work is managed to produce benefits with maximum efficiency and minimum variance.

> Measures of progress to plan in units of physical percent complete.

  • Tangible evidence of "working products" or "acceptable service" must be produced at planned intervals, short enough to take corrective actions when variances appear.

> Risks are "managed" using standard approaches.

  • All numbers—cost, schedule, technical performance—are considered random numbers with known variance.

  • Managing in the presence of the variances is the foundation of any credible risk management plan.

CHAPTER 2

The Five Immutable Principles of Project Success

Project failure starts when we can't tell what "done" looks like in any meaningful way. Without some agreement on our vision of "done", we'll never recognize it when it arrives, except when we've run out of time or money or both.

We've all seen the project failure numbers before.[1] We've all been told how bad things are. We've all heard that large numbers of projects fail because of poor planning or poor project management. Whether this is true or not, how can we increase the probability of our own project's success?

First, we must recognize that without a clear and concise description of done, the only measures of progress are the passage of time, consumption of resources, and production of technical features. These measures of progress fail to describe what business capabilities our project needs to produce or what mission we are trying to accomplish. In Chapter 1, we examined the ten drivers of project success, the first of which is that capabilities drive requirements. Therefore, without first identifying the needed capabilities, we cannot deliver a successful project, and we will end up a statistic like all the other failed projects.

With capabilities as our starting point, we're now going to look at the Five Immutable Principles of project success as they apply to any project, in any domain, using any project management method and any project management tool.

As we've seen, the Five Immutable Principles are best stated in the form of five questions. When we have the answers to these questions, we will have insight into the activities required for the project to succeed in ways not found using the traditional process group's checklist, knowledge areas, or canned project templates.

Before proceeding to the principles, let's remind ourselves of the attributes of projects. First, projects are one-off events. Projects are not operations. They are not repeatable processes—although the processes that manage projects are repeatable. A project is a one-time occurrence. This is important because projects are a "one chance to get it right" type of endeavor. Operations have several chances to get it right—maybe a lot of chances, sometimes only a few, but never just one. To increase a project's chances of success, the ten drivers, Five Immutable Principles, and Five Practices must all be followed.

Second, projects have many variables: some dependent, some independent, some we can control, and some we can't control. Three fundamental variables found in all projects are shown in Figure 2.1. These three variables interact in ways that are not easily discernible; however, we can ask three questions about them:

1. When will we be done?
2. How much will the project cost when it is done?
3. Will the deliverables from the project work when they arrive?

FIGURE 2.1 The three fundamental variables of projects.

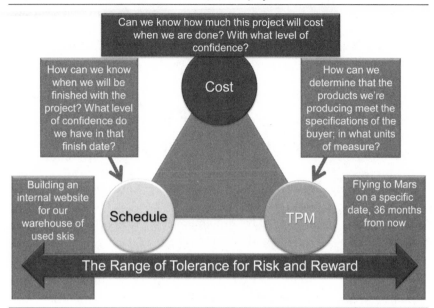

A word used in all project work is *probability*. Projects have statistical behaviors that drive how likely it is that they will succeed. There is no guarantee of success, of course. All projects' variables (cost, schedule, and technical performance) have associated uncertainties. As project managers, we'd like the probability of success to be as high as possible, and for some projects the probability of success is high—close to 100 percent. For some projects the probability of success, while acceptable, is actually low. The Five Immutable Principles focus on improving the Probability of Project Success (PoPS). The tradeoffs between risk and reward along the bottom of Figure 2.1 can now be seen in units of measure of cost, schedule, and technical performance. Risk becomes the common element between these three variables.

Another attribute common to all projects was suggested by Mr. Blaise Durante, Deputy Assistant Secretary (Acquisition and Integration) U.S. Air Force: *There are only two phases of any project ... (1) Too early to tell, and (2) Too late to stop.*[2]

All project managers want to have other choices. To do so, we need to answer the three questions in ways that provide actionable information to the decision makers, both project management and stakeholders. The Five Immutable Principles help us do that.

Implementing the
Five Immutable Principles

The Five Immutable Principles of project success are short and sweet. They are obvious, they are simple, and they are easily recognized. At the same time, they are hard to implement if we don't consciously and intentionally take the time and effort to do so.

1. **What does "done" look like?** We need to know where we are going by defining "done" for some point in the future. This may be far in the future—months or years—or closer—days or weeks from now.

2. **How can we get to "done" on time and on budget and achieve acceptable outcomes?** We need a plan to get to where we are going, to reach done. This plan can be simple or complex. The fidelity of the plan depends on our tolerance for risk. The complexity of the plan has to match the complexity of the project.

3. **Do we have enough of the right resources to successfully complete the project?** We have to understand what resources are needed to execute the plan. We need to know how much time and money are required to reach the destination. This can be fixed or it can be variable. If money is limited, the project may be possible if more time is available and vice versa. What technologies are needed? What information must be discovered that we don't know now?

4. **What impediments will we encounter along the way and what work is needed to remove them?** We need a means of removing, avoiding, handling, or ignoring these impediments.

Most important, we need to ask and answer the question, "How long are we willing to wait before we find out we are late?"

5. **How can we measure our progress to plan?** We need to measure planned progress, not just progress. Progress to plan is best measured in units of physical percent complete, which provides tangible evidence not just opinion. This evidence must be in "usable" outcomes that the buyer recognizes as the things they requested from the project.

When we hear the word *principles,* we might think about the principles of playing baseball.[3] Or the principles of garden design.[4] Principles are guidelines and must be put into practice with some reasonable hope of success. The principles must be based on practices that have been shown to work in the domain in which they are being applied. The Five Immutable Principles can be applied in all domains, where projects are the means of producing results. In Chapter 5, there are examples of practices—based on these principles—applied to actual projects in a variety of domains.

The Role of Risk in Project Management

This is an idea that is not considered enough when we think about processes and principles. The amount of risk a project can tolerate is directly related to the business domain and the context of the project within that domain. Understanding the tolerance for these risk levels is critical, for example, to choosing and applying any software development method. The risk tolerance for schedule slippage is defined as the ability to still produce value for the customer in the presence of a late or slipping schedule; the Boeing 787 Dreamliner is but one example. The risk tolerance for cost means the customer can handle an overrun and still consider the project a success; the Sydney Opera House is a case in point. The risk tolerance for technical performance shortfall means the customer is willing to accept technical capabilities that are less than planned—the original Windows 7 release exemplifies this. With this risk informed background, we can look at the Five Immutable Principles.

What "Done" Looks Like

Let's answer the first question from the point of view of the customer or the recipient of the outcomes of the project. For our purposes, the units of measure used to answer this question are the capabilities needed to meet the business mission goals. To reach "done," we need a plan and a schedule.

Our first step is to separate the plan from the schedule. The plan is a procedure used to achieve an objective. It is a set of intended actions through which one expects to achieve a goal. The schedule is the sequence of the intended actions needed to implement the plan.

The plan is a strategy for the successful completion of the project. In the strategic planning domain, a plan is a hypothesis that needs to be tested along the way to confirm we're headed in the right direction and will reach our goal.

The schedule is the order of the work that is needed to execute the plan. In project management, we need both. Plans without schedules are not executable. Schedules without plans lack a stated mission, vision, or description of success. All it says is that the work will be done.

Customers Buy Capabilities

Customers don't buy development methods. They don't buy requirements documents. They buy the plan because the answer to knowing what "done" looks like is described in the plan, and the customer is interested only in the final product. For that reason, the plan needs to answer the following questions:

> ➤ What capabilities are we seeking to deliver?

> ➤ What will the end user do with these capabilities that will create value for the business or fulfill a mission?

> ➤ What are the Measures of Effectiveness of these capabilities in units meaningful to the decision makers?[5]

> ➤ What is the sequence for the delivery of each capability and what are the incremental increases in the maturity of each capability needed to deliver value to the customer?

When we ask, "What does 'done' look like?" we should be referring to physical outcomes—the deliverables. By deliverables, we mean those things that enable the capabilities that fulfill the customer's requirements.

Frederick P. Brooks Jr. in his 1987 essay "No Silver Bullet: Essence and Accident in Software Engineering," said, "The hardest single part of building a system is deciding precisely what to build."[6]

No matter what method we use to decide what to build—from the agilest of methods to the most formal—the requirements need to be stated in a form that is testable, verifiable, and traceable to the plan and schedule and the needed capabilities.

Capabilities Produce Measurable Value

"Done" is defined by the Measures of Effectiveness—the operational measures of success that are closely related to the achievements of the mission or its operational objectives evaluated in the operational environment, under a specific set of conditions as determined by the buyer. They answer these questions:

> ➤ Does the outcome of the project meet the needs of the customer?

> ➤ What capability does the customer now have that wasn't there before?

> ➤ Does this new capability provide measurable value?

> ➤ If so, what is the evidence that this value was derived from the delivered products or services?

To be effective, a solution must address the user's Critical Operational Issues (COI), which are associated with "mission success." The COIs are the emergent properties of the solution that must be delivered to the customer for it to serve its function. If the solution does not have these characteristics, then it has not addressed the user's needs and is therefore unacceptable. COIs are "show stoppers" in the real sense of the term, as they are the emergent properties that a solution to a need must possess in order to meet the need.

The Plan Shows the Capabilities' Increasing Maturity

Figure 2.2 is an actual project's master plan. This plan is for a healthcare insurance firm that is deploying a new provider network system. It begins with the development of a pilot system that integrates some test data and demonstrates that the conversion process for member reconciliation can be done as planned.

> ➤ This plan includes several concepts not usually found in a traditional project management approach, the first of which is that it starts with the requirements. A master plan is developed up front to provide the needed business capabilities before moving on to anything else in the project. In this case, it allows us to confirm that the pilot system can convert the data contained in the previous application to the new system.

> ➤ This work verifies the increasing "maturity" of the project's deliverables; that is, the technical requirements are present, and we have a capability, possibly a small capability—that we can perform the conversion—which moves the maturity of the project one step higher.

> ➤ The master plan contains all the steps needed to increase the maturity of the project as defined at the project's outset. This does not mean we know all the details of "how" we are going to get to "done," but it does show what "done" looks like at the end of the project. In Figure 2.2, this is labeled Phase 1 Go Live.

The next step in the master plan after Phase 1, Go Live, is to integrate the enrollment subsystem. With this capability, using the pilot system and the legacy data, new providers can be enrolled. Add the integrators, the quality monitor, and the billing components and the first set of capabilities can be put to work.

Some might say this is just like Agile. That's true, but the plan doesn't say anything about developing software, features, stories, a schedule, or anything about developing products. It states in clear and concise terms what capabilities are needed in what order, and what the dependencies are among those capabilities. Notice the focus on "capabilities." It's the capability that the customer bought, not the development method, the

FIGURE 2.2 This master plan lays out needed business capabilities for an insurance provider network system.

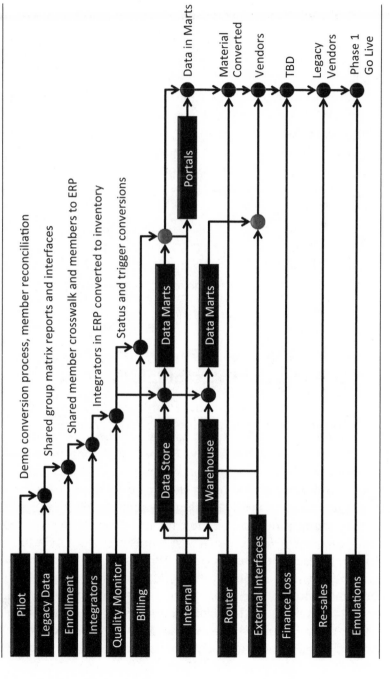

code, or even the processes wrapped around most software or product development methods. These are all necessary but far from sufficient for project success.

To summarize:

> ➤ Customers buy capabilities. These capabilities are implemented by products or services, but it is the capabilities that deliver the business value.

> ➤ To find out what capabilities are needed, an elicitation process must be conducted before anything else is done on the project. Without knowing what capabilities are needed, we cannot know what "done" looks like.

> ➤ For each capability, we need a Measure of Effectiveness. We'll get to the details of MoEs in Chapter 3, but, for now, the MoE is the tangible evidence that the project is delivering the business or mission value the customer needs to call the project a success.

How to Get to "Done" on Time and on Budget with Acceptable Outcomes

Once we know what capabilities need to be provided to the customer, in what order these capabilities are provided, and what the dependencies are among the capabilities, we will know what "done" looks like, as shown in Figure 2.2.

Figure 2.3 will be referred to in the following chapters. Along with Figure 2.2, it is the basis for managing any project. Together they describe two critical processes needed for any project's success. Each planned capability in Figure 2.2 can be represented as a milestone or event in Figure 2.3. The integration of the enrollment processes with the Enterprise Resource Planning (ERP) system can be a milestone. So can the conversion of all the legacy materials. We can define any usable deliverable as a milestone. The milestone or event represents the ability to do something useful with the deliverables of the project. The best useful thing is to put them to work. Process orders, make a product, fly to some destination without passengers in our new vehicle, but fly just the same. There needs to be some tangible evidence that the project is capable of producing value for the customer on the planned day for the planned cost.

For the milestone to be met, we need to accomplish something that produces the value. These accomplishments are the entry criteria for delivering the capability. They are what enables the capability to exist. For each accomplishment, one or more "criteria" is used to assess the "done-ness" of the work performed to produce a product or a service.

The actual work that takes place on the project is contained in work packages, which hold the work activities, the resources needed to perform the work, and the measures used to assess the progress of the work as it is performed.

All three elements—milestones, accomplishment, and criteria—need to be in place before we can talk about the success of the project. If we leave one out, we will also be leaving out a critical piece of information needed to assess each of the Five Immutable Principles and our Five Practices will be weakened.

Implementing the Work

The next step is to perform the work defined in the work packages shown in Figure 2.3. The work packages are where the project team defines its activities. Whether it is writing code, bending metal, shoveling dirt, developing a drug, or teaching a class, they are all implemented through "work packages."

The work packages contain the scheduled activities needed to reach "done." This is where the actual work takes place to produce products or services. Figure 2.3 shows how these work packages are connected to another important element of our Five Immutable Principles—the work breakdown structure. We'll examine the WBS further in Chapter 3, but for now, it is important to note that the WBS is a deconstruction of all the products and services needed to produce the deliverables for the project. The terminal nodes of this WBS are work packages that produce the project's deliverables. In turn, these deliverables implement the capabilities for the stakeholders.

FIGURE 2.3 Work packages define specific activities leading to a capability.

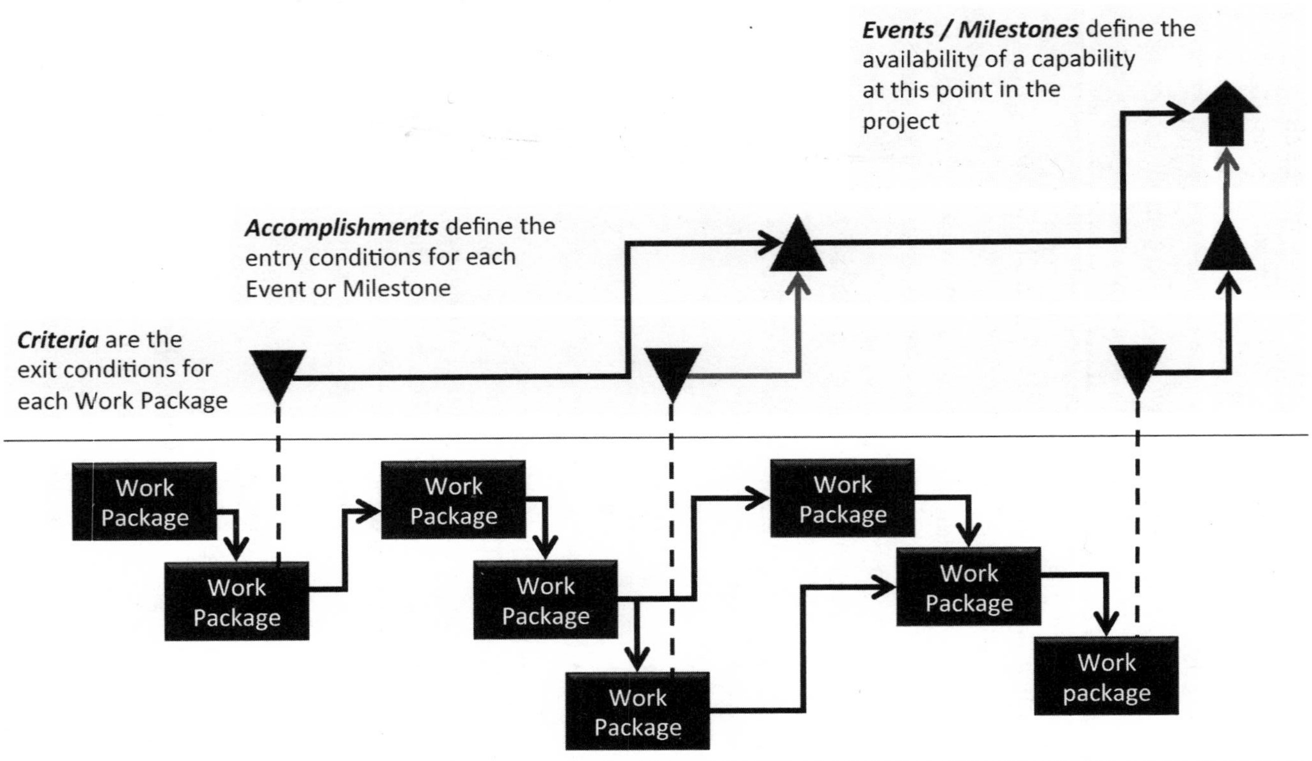

Events / Milestones define the availability of a capability at this point in the project

Accomplishments define the entry conditions for each Event or Milestone

Criteria are the exit conditions for each Work Package

to some destination without passengers in our new vehicle, but fly just the same. There needs to be some tangible evidence that the project is capable of producing value for the customer on the planned day for the planned cost.

For the milestone to be met, we need to accomplish something that produces the value. These accomplishments are the entry criteria for delivering the capability. They are what enables the capability to exist. For each accomplishment, one or more "criteria" is used to assess the "done-ness" of the work performed to produce a product or a service.

The actual work that takes place on the project is contained in work packages, which hold the work activities, the resources needed to perform the work, and the measures used to assess the progress of the work as it is performed.

All three elements—milestones, accomplishment, and criteria—need to be in place before we can talk about the success of the project. If we leave one out, we will also be leaving out a critical piece of information needed to assess each of the Five Immutable Principles and our Five Practices will be weakened.

Implementing the Work

The next step is to perform the work defined in the work packages shown in Figure 2.3. The work packages are where the project team defines its activities. Whether it is writing code, bending metal, shoveling dirt, developing a drug, or teaching a class, they are all implemented through "work packages."

The work packages contain the scheduled activities needed to reach "done." This is where the actual work takes place to produce products or services. Figure 2.3 shows how these work packages are connected to another important element of our Five Immutable Principles—the work breakdown structure. We'll examine the WBS further in Chapter 3, but for now, it is important to note that the WBS is a deconstruction of all the products and services needed to produce the deliverables for the project. The terminal nodes of this WBS are work packages that produce the project's deliverables. In turn, these deliverables implement the capabilities for the stakeholders.

While building a plan that delivers the needed capabilities, we also need to build a credible WBS. There are numerous books and resources that explain how to build a good work breakdown structure, but there are underlying principles that guide the development of a WBS. The WBS is a necessary project element and is defined, developed, and maintained throughout the system life cycle based on the disciplined application of a systems engineering process.

Some important attributes of a WBS are that it:

> - Is a product-oriented family tree composed of hardware, software, services, data, and facilities

> - Displays and defines the product(s) to be developed and/or produced

> - Illustrates the elements of work to be accomplished and relates them to each other and to the end product

Another critical attribute of a WBS is the MECE (mutually exclusive, collectively exhaustive) principle:

> - **Mutually Exclusive (ME).** No subcategory should represent any other subcategory ("no overlaps"). In the WBS, this means the deliverables are unique so we can assign cost to them and determine who is going to develop them.

> - **Collectively Exhaustive (CE).** All subcategories, taken together, should fully characterize the larger category of which the data are part ("no gaps"). The WBS represents the "all-in" work. If it's not in the WBS, it is not going to get done.

Building a good WBS does not start with defining the level of the WBS. It starts with the MECE principle and the resulting product (or service) architecture.

WBS building is systems architecture, in the same way technical design is systems architecture, for several reasons:

> - We need to know which of the system's components are mutually exclusive.

➤ The subcategories of these components must be collectively exhaustive. Parts can be shared in the WBS, if the work for those parts can be shared, but they need to be assigned different WBS numbers, so it is clear that they are ME at the same time as they are CE.

➤ The WBS can then be used to collect costs and answer the questions, "What does this part, subassembly, assembly, or system cost, and where does it fit in the overall project?"

➤ The resources (one of the Five Immutable Principles) are then assigned (not named by categories—names change when control changes; names of categories don't change) and the Responsibility Assignment Matrix (RAM) built to see who is working on what, and at what cost.

How to Assess Resources

Now that we know where we want to go, the next question is how to get there. How do we build the products or provide the services needed to reach the end of our project? There are numerous choices, depending on the domain and the context of the project in that domain.

All resources—internal and external, their dependencies, and any other items needed to produce the deliverables—are defined in the work packages. The work package manager is accountable for managing all these resources. If resources are not under the control of the work package manager, the risk to the success of the deliverables is increased because accountability is no longer traceable to a single person—violating the principles of the Responsibility Assignment Matrix. The RAM assigns accountability for each deliverable to a single person. In some development paradigms, there is shared accountability, but this is trouble waiting to happen. A single point of integrative responsibility is a critical success factor. That person can certainly "share" responsibility, but accountability is singular.

Planning for Resources

Planning the resources for a project starts with a Resource Management Plan. This is a written plan, driven by the work packages, stating the types of resources, number needed, and their need date.

This plan needs to address:

> **The Demand Forecast.** With the work package "owners" in the room, a full-time equivalent (FTE) demand model must be built. How many hours of work are planned for the work package? In the workweek plan, how many full-time staff does this translate into? This approach does not address (yet) productivity, specialty skills, availability of these skills, facilities, tools, or any other item needed for success.

> **Existing or Proposed Resources.** There needs to be an assessment of the on-hand resources, their availability, and their "effectiveness." This is the first time we consider how effective the current resources are and how that effectiveness affects our project.

> **Planning Assumptions.** This stage of the plan is the start of risk management. Assumptions are those things that may or may not come true, those things that need to come true for the project to be a success, and those things that can't happen if the project is going to be a success. Thus, Assumption-Based Planning asks questions about what the future might look like.[7]

> **Future Resources.** A forecast of future resource needs can be made in conjunction with the demand for resources in the form of an FTE model, the currently available resources, and the assumptions about the future demands for not only resources, but all aspects of the project. This is a probabilistic forecast indicating a confidence level for the needed resources. We'll talk more about probabilistic forecasting, risk, and performance measures in Chapter 5 when we discuss Continuous Risk Management processes.

> **An Integrated Resource Plan.** Now we can start to build the Resource Management Plan. There are many templates on the web

for this. Minimally, the plan contains a list of resources needed once you have assessed your demand, the availability of current resources, and the assumptions around those needs. Once you have assessed these, the equipment, facilities, and all the other nonpersonnel resources are assessed and planned.

> ➤ **Short-Term "Call to Action" Plan.** With the Resource Management Plan in hand, it is time to execute the plan.

How to Handle
Impediments and Assess Risk

Project managers constantly seek ways to eliminate or control risk, variance, and uncertainty. This is a hopeless pursuit. Managing "in the presence" of risk, variance, and uncertainty is the key to success. Some projects have few uncertainties—only the complexity of tasks and relationships is important—but most projects are characterized by several types of uncertainty. Although each uncertainty in our project domain is distinct, a single project may encounter some combination of the four classes of uncertainty:[8]

1. **Natural Variation.** These uncertainties come from many small influences and yield a range of values on a particular activity. Attempting to control these variances outside their natural boundaries is a waste. This type of uncertainty is labeled *aleatory* (variance-based risk) and is "naturally" occurring. It is part of the process, the culture. It's just "in the air." The key here is that it is not possible to reduce aleatory uncertainty. The only protection is to have cost, schedule, and technical "margin" to absorb these variances.

2. **Foreseen Uncertainty.** These uncertainties are identifiable and understood influences that the team cannot be sure will occur. There must be a mitigation plan for them. This type of uncertainty is labeled *epistemic* (event-based risk). The probability that a specific risk will occur can be created. This type of uncertainty

and resulting risk can be "handled" in two ways. First, the risk can be "bought down," or "retired," by spending money to learn more information or doing work to remove the uncertainty and therefore the risk. Second, management reserve can be provided to protect the project should this risk occur. Management reserve (MR) is the amount of the total budget withheld for management control purposes, rather than assigned for the accomplishment of work. MR is held and applied through a disciplined process to any additional work that is to be accomplished within the authorized work scope.

3. **Unforeseen Uncertainty.** These are uncertainties that can't be identified during project planning. When they occur, a new plan is needed to deal with the uncertainty and the resulting risk created by the unforeseen uncertainty.

4. **Chaos.** These uncertainties appear in the presence of "unknown unknowns" (UNK UNK). The concept of UNK UNK is overused and even abused. "We didn't see it coming" is a common response. In fact, we were just too lazy to look for the risk. Our mortgage crisis, our lack of understanding of international politics, and our failure to adequately talk to the stakeholders are all examples of the misapplication of UNK UNKs.

Both of these uncertainties are related to three aspects of our project management domain:

1. **The External World.** These are the activities of the project that are impacted by events and processes outside the project (e.g., the weather, vendor performance, prices of materials, politics, and business cycles).

2. **Our Knowledge of This World.** These are the planned and actual behaviors of the project as we can detect them from observations, research, and analysis.

3. **Our Perception of This World.** These are the data and information we receive about these behaviors and how we interpret the data when making decisions about the risk created by the uncertainty.

There are consistent themes that contribute to the "less than accept-able" outcomes for projects that must be addressed by risk management:[9]

> ➤ Significant gaps in the risk management practices employed by programs and organizations

> ➤ Uneven and inconsistent application of risk management prac-tices within and across organizations

> ➤ Ineffective integration of risk management with program and or-ganizational management

> ➤ Increasingly complex management environment

Each of these can be found on projects that got into trouble. The solutions are obvious in principle but hard in practice because the foun-dation for success was not laid in the beginning. Correcting troubled projects—triage—is difficult. It is much easier to start the project cor-rectly by applying the Five Immutable Principles than to add them later to a troubled project.

Plans for Handling Risk

For the project to increase its probability of success, both uncertainty types—aleatory and epistemic—must be "handled." The risk resulting from the uncertainties are first recorded in a Risk Register, along with the plans for handling them, the variances for the naturally occurring uncertainties, and probability of occurrence for the foreseen risks. The Risk Register is then assessed for its impact on cost and schedule. We need to determine the management reserve we are willing to commit to cover the known uncertainties and the resulting risk. We also need to determine how much schedule and cost margin we want to carry in the Integrated Master Schedule (IMS). The IMS is a term used on large complex projects. It contains all the work to be performed, the specific deliverables, and the planned budget to produce those deliverables. In Chapter 3, we'll take a deeper dive into building the IMS. With these numbers, we then need to determine any residual risks and if there is sufficient budget and time to handle them should they also occur.

How to Measure Progress to Plan

Measuring progress is difficult on many projects. Some start by measuring how much was spent on the work performed. This, of course, just tells us if we're on budget at any given point in the project. Sometimes, progress is measured by the passage of time. The current duration of the project divided by the total duration gives us the "percent complete." These are all necessary measures of progress, but they are far from sufficient in support of the Five Immutable Principles. None of these measurements speak to what was actually done on the project in terms of our movement toward "done." We know from earlier in this chapter that "done" is defined by the capabilities delivered by the project, whose units are MoEs. With the information from the four immutable principles already discussed, we now need to confirm that we are making actual progress, not just spending money and passing time with our fifth principle.

The key principle here is "planned progress." We must predefine what progress we need to make at any specific point in the project, otherwise all we can determine is how much time has passed and how much money has been consumed. Preplanning progress is the basis of "performance-based" measurement for both project processes and technical products. As Kent Beck said, "Optimism is the disease of development, feedback is the cure."[10] We need tangible evidence through feedback on our progress. There is only one kind of feedback for projects—measures of physical percent complete. No soft touchy-feely measures of progress. No hand-waving measures. We need physical, tangible evidence of progress. Something we can actually show to the customer. Something that is compliant with the planned technical outcomes at this point in the plan. Figure 2.4 shows the connections between the measures needed for these principles.

These measures are independent of any product development methodology. For our measures of progress to plan on any project, we need to have the following:

> ➤ "Tangible evidentiary materials," which means that there is proof of progress, not just someone stating that progress has been made.

FIGURE 2.4 The work breakdown structure shows how progress is measured.

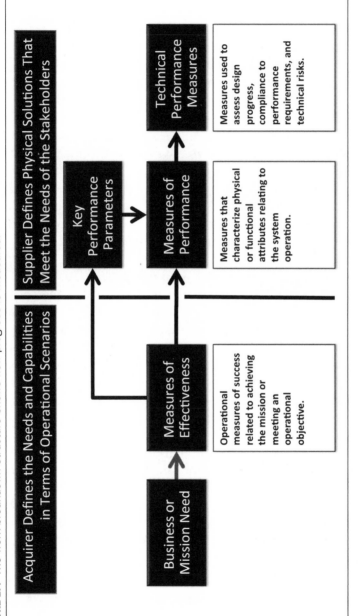

> Predefined existence of this evidence in meaningful units of measure established *before* work began. For example, if we wanted to use the weight of a bridge design as a measure of performance, we'd have our CAD model tell us the ranges of weights from the 3D solid structures model to be used to assess the final design weight.

> Progress defined in these same units of measure.

We'll see in Chapter 5 how to put the measures in Figure 2.4 to work. Here, we will look a little closer at each measure.

> **Business or Mission Need.** This measure is a description of what capabilities the business needs to possess in order for the project to be successful. These capabilities state what "done" looks like in some form that is meaningful to the customer. For example, if we wanted to replace a transaction processing system with a cheaper one, we would define the target transaction costs before we started the development to ensure that everyone knows what "done" looks like.

> **Measures of Effectiveness.** These are the operational measures of success that are closely related to the achievements of the mission or operational objectives evaluated in the operational environment, under a specific set of conditions.

> **Measures of Performance.** These measures characterize physical or functional attributes relating to the system operation, measured or estimated under specific conditions.

> **Key Performance Parameters.** These measures represent the capabilities and characteristics so significant that failure to meet them can be cause for reevaluation, reassessment, or termination of the program.

> **Technical Performance Measures.** These measures are attributes that determine how well a system or element of a system is satisfying or expected to satisfy a technical requirement or goal.

Measuring Planned Progress

Measuring progress alone is not sufficient to increase the probability of success. We need to measure progress made against planned progress. To do this, we must have defined what progress we should have made, using the measures in Figure 2.4, on a defined day or for a defined period of performance. This means that before the project can be successful, we need to know what "done" looks like in these four measures—Effectiveness, Performance, Key Performance Parameters, and Technical Performance. Without these, we will return to measuring progress to plan using the passage of time and consumption of resources.

Like our uncertainty and risk assessment, these measures of progress are probabilistic. They are driven by the underlying statistical process, and the margin of error should be indicated. It is not to correct to say we want to decrease the cost of process transactions; we need to say what the tolerance on the target value is. Is it $0.07 exactly, or $0.07 ± 5 percent?

Then we need to speak about these measures in confidence intervals. How confident are we that we can reduce the transaction cost to $0.07? Is it 90 percent confidence, 80 percent confidence? It cannot be 100 percent since projects are probabilistic "beasts" and no variable is deterministic.

A critical point here is that when someone provides you with a single point estimate, and doesn't provide the margin of error or the level of confidence, then by default, it can't be right.

Looking Back

In Chapter 1, we looked at the drivers of project success—the activities and the artifacts or the elements that pushed the project along its path to completion. In this chapter, we developed the notion of Five Immutable Principles based on those drivers. These principles are the foundation of successful projects in any domain, using any project management method, and any product development process. The project can test if the principles are being applied by asking five questions. Without credible answers to the five questions, the probability of success for the project is reduced.

Let's ask the questions for the Five Immutable Principles again in slightly expanded form and examine what credible answers might be:

1. Do we know what "done" looks like in units of measure meaningful to the decision makers?

   > Done needs to be measured as the capabilities provided to the buyer. These capabilities are derived from the business or mission needs. The capabilities provide the business or organization with the "ability" to do something new, something in support of its strategy.

     - In our new insurance claims management system we need the capability to pre-process insurance claims at $0.07 per transaction rather than the current $0.11 per transaction.

     - On our service mission to the Hubble Space Telescope, we need the capability to change the Wide Field Camera and the internal nickel hydride batteries, while doing no harm to the telescope.

     - We need the capability to comply with new procurement regulations for selling to the federal government using the current ERP system and the supporting work processes in ways we have not done before.

   > These capabilities are measured by their effectiveness to meet the needs of the buyer, either in terms of business effectiveness or mission effectiveness.

     - The target of $0.07 per transaction will have lower bound of $0.06 and upper bound of $0.08 in a probability distribution. No transaction cost processed by the business rules will exceed $0.09 without manual intervention.

     - After installation of the Wide Field Camera during Service Mission 4, the UVIS Field of Vision will be restored to <0.00014 e-/pix/s.

     - Starting with our old procurement system (Catalog Sales), migrate all baseline cost of goods to the new procurement system (Engineer to Order) with 100 percent accuracy, within one accounting period, and provide customers access to the data at the start of the next business month.

> Successful project managers have a list of what capabilities are needed from the project for the customer, the units of measure of these capabilities, and where in the sequence of work each of these capabilities will be delivered and ready to use.

  • Using an approach similar to that shown in Figure 2.2, document each milestone and support deliverables in a Concept of Operations or similar document.[11]

2. Do we have a plan to reach "done" on time and on budget?

> Our plan has to describe how we are going to deliver each capability and how we are going to measure the increasing maturity of that capability as it emerges from our work effort.

  • A step-by-step migration plan at the top-level deliverables starts with a pilot that imports provider data and applies the new enrollment process. This will demonstrate that the legacy system data have integrity in the new system.

  • Using the Wide Field Camera 3 Instrument Mini-Handbook Cycle 16 operations plan, define the integration and test data target results in work packages for each test suite.

  • Define a product capability roadmap, describing the user interface for procurement and warehouse material pull processes that match the "engineer to order" guidance in FAR 15.

> Our plan is connected to the sequence of work activities that will produce the outcomes from the project. This work sequence is usually called a "schedule," but it can also be called other things, as long as it states the order of work and the evidence that the work is producing an outcome.

  • Using the structure of the plan in Figure 2.1 and Figure 2.2, construct a sequence of properly linked work packages to define the master schedule, with durations, resources, and risk retirement activities. Budget and resources are assigned to the work packages, making this a candidate to start the project. Changes always occur and, if accepted, are reflected in the schedule.

> ➤ Successful project managers have a plan and a schedule for producing the deliverables on the planned date, for the planned cost, with planned technical compliance to the specifications.

3. Do we know what resources we need to reach "done"?

> ➤ Resources mean anything that we use during the project—people, facilities, consumables, external items.

> > • Resource assignment starts at the work package level and any conflicts resolve before starting the initial work. The work package manager initiates the resource-loading plan by identifying how many full-time equivalents (FTEs) are needed.

> ➤ The timing, location, quality, capabilities, capacity, and other attributes of these resources must be aligned with the need for them. This means there must be a plan for these resources similar to a plan for the project outcomes.

> > • With the rough head count, skills and availability can be planned. This is an iterative process and cannot be skipped.

4. Do we know what impediments we'll encounter along the way to "done," and how we are going to handle them?

> ➤ Uncertainty is part of all projects. Managing in the presence of uncertainty is what project managers do.

> > • Managing risk starts and ends with the Risk Register, which contains the risk name, the probability of occurrence (for event-based risks), the cost impact if the risk "come true," the cost of handling, the residual risk after handling, the probability of occurrence for the residual risk, the cost of handling the residual risk, and the impacts on work packages and deliverables.

> Uncertainty creates risk. Managing in the presence of risk means having a plan for how to handle both the uncertainty and the resulting risk.

  • Along with event-based risk (epistemic uncertainty), there is variance-based risk (aleatory uncertainty). Aleatory uncertainty creates schedule slippage and cost growth due to naturally occurring processes. No actual work ever takes "exactly" the planned duration. Materials, labor, and equipment have cost variances that must be considered. Aleatory uncertainty and risk are handled with margin or management reserve; for example schedule margin, cost margin, management reserve for "in scope" but unplanned outcomes.

5. Do we know how we are going to measure progress to plan in terms of physical percent complete?

> Measuring progress to plan requires tangible evidence. These provide measures of physical percent complete.

  • The number of providers migrated from the legacy systems to the new provider system along with the data and the ability to enroll clients.

  • The passing of the Built-in Testing of the camera's on-board data processing systems that create JPEG images for return to Earth.

  • Verification that product orders can be passed through the system and compliance with business rules verified for a statistically sampled set of parts.

> Opinion, professional judgment, the passage of time, or consumption of resources are not measures of progress.

  • Physically observing the claims processing system work on a "test suite" of data in the new system.

  • Physically testing the camera's capabilities and reporting the results on the test for the engineering staff to assess.

  • Physical evidence of purchase orders and warehouse "pulls" for the sample data set.

> ➤ Only measures of physical percent complete against the planned physical percent complete at the planned time in the project are measures of progress.

What's Ahead?

With the Five Immutable Principles in place, let's move on to the Five Practices needed to increase the probability of project success:

1. Identify the capabilities needed to achieve the project objectives.

2. Elicit technical and operational requirements needed for system capabilities to be fulfilled.

3. Establish a Performance Measurement Baseline for the time-phased network of activities needed to produce the project's outcomes.

4. Execute the Performance Measurement Baseline, while ensuring that technical performance is met, risks are retired, and the needed capabilities are delivered.

5. Apply Continuous Risk Management to each work activity to ensure that the identified uncertainties and resulting risks are properly handled.

CHAPTER 3

The Five Immutable Practices of Project Success

With the Five Immutable Principles in place, let's put them to work by implementing the Five Immutable Practices. Each of the Five Practices, like the Five Principles, is needed for project success. There are no shortcuts to success, so no skipping any practice.

The foundation of the Performance-Based Project Management method is the integration of the Five Practices with the Five Principles. These activities must be performed by project managers and participants to increase the probability of project success.

In the end, we must always remember that project management is about making decisions in the presence of uncertainty. Managing in the presence of uncertainty starts with the steps, outcomes, and benefits described in Figure 3.1.

Implementing the Five Immutable Practices

The Five Practices may seem obvious, but the obvious is not always found in the project domain. If it was, more projects would be successful. Figure 3.1 shows the Five Practices, their relationships to one another, and the top-level outcomes that are needed to increase the probability of any project's success. Each practice creates outcomes used by the following practice. Each practice creates outcomes used as feedback to the others. The first four practices are supported by the fifth, Continuous Risk Management. Every action done in the first four must be assessed for explicit and latent risks to the success of the project.

As Figure 3.1 illustrates, the Five Practices needed to implement the Five Immutable Principles are:

1. **Identify the needed capabilities.** This is the first and most important practice—the discovery of what capabilities are needed for the success of the project. To achieve the project's objectives or a particular end state, we need to define these capabilities. We do this through scenarios from the customer's point of view, using the customer's Measure of Effectiveness (MoE) in units meaningful to the decision maker. Effectiveness measures describe how well the results from the project enable a business process or fulfill a strategic mission of the business.

2. **Identify the baseline requirements.** Define both technical and operational requirements that will fulfill the needed capabilities; stipulate the planned time, the planned cost, and the planned technical performance of the resulting product or service. This means every requirement is traceable to work, all work is traceable to at least one requirement, and each requirement

FIGURE 3.1 The Five Immutable Practices identify desired outcomes and provide opportunities for feedback.

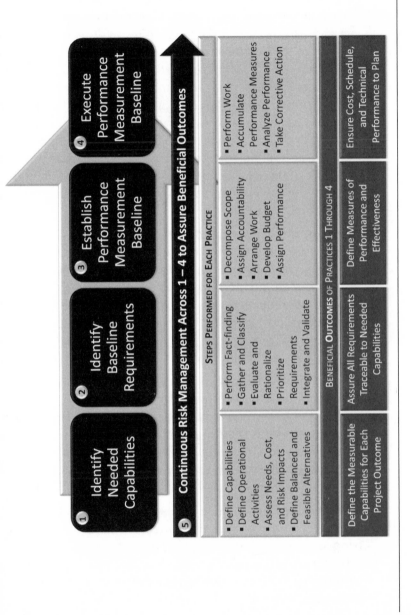

is traceable to each capability. The baseline requirements must be defined in terms isolated from any implementation, technical products, or processes. Only then can we bind the requirements with a technology. This means the managers of the project should wait as long as possible to determine the technical solution to the requirements. Only when the requirements have been defined and traced back to the needed capabilities should candidates for the technical solution be considered. If this decision is made too soon, the commitment to a specific technology may constrain alternative solutions. These requirements are assessed using their Measures of Performance (MoP) in fulfilling the Measures of Effectiveness to then provide value to the customers' business or mission; in other words, we must determine whether the requirements we've established will actually meet the customers' need.

3. **Develop the Performance Measurement Baseline (PMB).** Once we have established the capabilities and requirements, we can determine the sequence of the work, the budget for this work, the outcomes from the work effort, the Measures of Performance, and the risk-reduction activities for each outcome that ensures progress is being made as planned. This PMB is our guide for managing the project. It is not cast in stone, but it is a map to "done." And like all maps, it needs to be reevaluated along the way.

4. **Execute the Performance Measurement Baseline.** Take each element of work and perform it in the planned order, ensuring that all work is completed successfully before proceeding to the next element. During execution, we measure project performance through adherence to cost, schedule, and Technical Performance Measures (TPM),[1] and their supporting Key Performance Parameters (KPP).[2]

5. **Perform Continuous Risk Management.** During each of the four preceding practices we'll need to manage risk by identifying, analyzing, planning, tracking, controlling, and communicating each technical and programmatic risk, and then taking corrective actions to reduce risk and increase the probability of the project's success.

A Framework for the Five Immutable Practices

Each of the Five Practices, guided by the Five Immutable Principles, performs a specific function in our efforts to increase the Probability of Project Success (PoPS). Like the principles, the practices are not a cafeteria-style approach, from which you can pick and choose what to apply to the project.

Each practice contains specific steps needed to produce measurable outcomes to increase the PoPS. If a practice is missing or poorly applied, the PoPS will be reduced, possibly in ways not known until the project is too far along to be recovered. Each practice provides actionable information needed to make management decisions about the project and its deliverables. This actionable information is the feedback mechanism needed to keep a project under control and on track. These control processes are not impediments to progress; they are the tools needed to increase the probability of success.

Identify the Needed Capabilities

Capabilities describe what must be successfully delivered to achieve the project's objectives or the particular end state for a specific scenario.

A capability provides the ability to do something using the project's outcome that has a recognized and verifiable benefit. Often, the management of a project begins with requirements, technology, tools, and the process and people that apply the technology and tools. But the customer doesn't actually buy features and functions. The customer buys a capability to do something of value. This can be a business value, a public service, or the completion of a mission. But the capability must have a verifiable value, recognized by all who participate in or benefit from the project. This measure of value has to be in units recognizable by the project's participants.

Without knowing what capabilities we need at the end of the project, the requirements, and everything else around managing the project has no home, no reason for being, and no connection to the actual goal of the project. The goal of any project must be to produce the capabilities needed to get something useful done and measure those capabilities through the value delivered to the buyer of the project's products or services.

These identified capabilities tell us what "done" looks like. Many project management methods skip this capabilities capture process and start by eliciting requirements; this is a mistake[3] because if the capabilities capture process is omitted, the participants in the project only know what "done" looks like in terms of time, money spent, and the technical features produced because the key connection—the connection to the business or mission—was never made. The result is usually disappointment on all fronts—time, cost, and outcomes.

Instead of starting with requirements, we need to start with capabilities that describe "done" in Measures of Effectiveness for the outcomes of the project, not just delivery of solutions derived from the requirements. These MoEs are operational measures of success related to the achievement of the mission or operational objectives under a specific set of conditions.

Here is how to develop capabilities and their Measures of Effectiveness:

> **Describe the solutions needed to achieve a business or mission objective.** Knowing the objectives is the starting point. With the stated objectives, the needed capabilities can be identified.

> **Connect the capabilities to the solution in units meaningful to the decision maker.** The end users of the project outcomes rarely care how the capabilities are delivered as long as those capabilities fulfill the technical and operational requirements.

> **Focus on measurable beneficial outcomes, independent of any technical implementation.** This allows a capability to be delivered in a variety of ways, providing freedom for the implementers to choose innovative, efficient, and effective solutions. If we choose the technical solution too soon, we are locked into a path that restricts innovation, streamlining, or even responding to changing requirements.

> ➤ **Connect the capabilities to mission success.** In the end, the customers didn't buy a technology, they bought a solution to a problem. Capabilities are not the requirements for the technology or the operations of the project's outcomes.

Four steps are needed to determine the capabilities necessary for the success of a project. Like the other practices in the Performance-Based Project Management method, the steps to identify the needed capabilities are performed in a logical sequence, each with a measurable outcome that allow us to evaluate the increasing maturity of the deliverables needed for project success.

Let's look at the four steps for identifying the needed capabilities.

Step 1 Define the Operational Concepts of the Project's Deliverables

We need to answer the question, "What is the system going to do when it is complete?" We'll start with the Concept of Operations (ConOps), which is a written or graphic statement that clearly and concisely shows what the stakeholders intended to accomplish through their mission or business strategy. The ConOps describes how these capabilities will be employed by the business to solve a problem or meet a business goal, and what benefits result when the project is "done."

This sounds a lot like goals and objectives, or maybe a strategy, or even some business optimization process. Those are closely connected to the ConOps, but the key to the ConOps is to define what the outcomes of the project will provide, in units of measure meaningful to the decision makers. This means some measure of how effective the outcome will be at doing its job.

The ConOps describes the problem to be solved, the classes of users, and the operational scenarios that show what the system is doing.[4] For example, the ConOps for an insurance transaction processing system would include all the possible transactions that would be processed, the staff needed for this processing, the procedures used to process them under normal conditions and any exceptions to those conditions, the number of transactions per day, and so on. The ConOps is the narrative description of what "done" looks like from the users' point of view.

We can then break down the ConOps into a Statement of Work (SOW), Statement of Objectives (SOO), or maybe even a Request for Proposal (RFP). This is done through a top-to-bottom trace of the concepts that connects each requirement with a ConOps element. This structure is a "map" of the needed capabilities and their interrelationships. It forms the basis of the requirements flow-down process that we'll see in the next step.

We need to start at the beginning of the project to capture capabilities in a form that can be used to trace requirements, deliverables, and performance measures back to these capabilities and define the MoEs for each capability. For example: "We need the capability to complete 95 percent of work on or before 15 business days or the negotiated deadline." MoPs are the criteria used to organize these MoEs. Measures of Performance are qualitative or quantitative measures of system capabilities or characteristics as seen from the provider's point of view. MoPs are broad physical and performance parameters, derived from the MoE. The basis of physical percent complete can be defined with MoPs, be traceable to the MoEs, and then traced to the needed capabilities.

The notion of physical percent complete is critical to the success of any project management method. Physical percent complete provides tangible evidence of progress to plan. It can be seen, touched, demonstrated, and observed in a predefined manner. The fact that it is "tangible" and "predefined" is the thing that is important. Use tangible evidence, not personal opinions—which are subjective—about how much progress has actually been made with objective proof.

Step 2   Define the Scenarios and Use Cases

Next, we need to answer the question, "How is are the business or stakeholders going to use the system, what actions can they take, and what are the results of these actions?" For each capability, we need a scenario and the use cases that fulfill the scenario. A use case is a list of steps, typically defining interactions between a role and the system, to achieve a goal from this system. These describe the sequence of the activities, who is performing them, and what the inputs and outputs are from these activities. This means that we must think through what we are going to do with the outcomes of the project in terms meaningful to the users.

One way to do this is to build a Value Stream Map (VSM) of the work processes of the outcomes and connect each scenario and use case to some point on the map to show how each capability provides value. The concept of the VSM originated at Toyota, where it was called *material and information flow*. It can be applied to any value chain. Our project example in Figure 2.2 is the "value chain" for the provider enrollment process at a health insurance firm. Value Stream Maps are typically found in manufacturing and information flows to identify products or services. Figure 2.2 is an example of a VSM for the delivered capabilities of the provider enrollment process for the health insurance claims processing system.

To build this map or something like it to show the increasing ability of the deliverables to meet the needed capabilities, we need to:

> ➤ List individual capabilities in the form of scenarios described through use cases, process flows, or operational descriptions.

> ➤ Assess the dependencies between the needed capabilities by identifying the "implicit" relationships. These are the dependencies that will cause trouble later. "I didn't know there was a connection," is the classic response. These implicit dependencies need to be made explicit for the capabilities description to be credible.

Step 3   Assess the Needed Capabilities

With our list of needed capabilities, we can ask and answer, "How will we measure the benefits of the resulting capabilities?" The questions are about schedule, cost, risk, and how they relate to the capabilities, and they need to be asked all at the same time. For example, if we are remodeling our kitchen, we need to ask when the appliances will be needed on site for installation. What preconditions will be needed to allow the appliances to be installed and put to use by the homeowner? This brings into focus a concept critical to the success of all projects.

Before we can know what something is worth, we have to know what it costs and how much risk we are willing to take for that cost to produce the capability. We need to know this if we are going to define what success looks like.

Our assessment of the needed capabilities must also make probabilistic estimates of schedule, risk, cost, and technical performance. It does us no good to state a cost number, or any number, in fact, without knowing the variances in the values of that number. It is common for business cases to contain dollar values for cost and benefit. But without knowing the variances on those numbers, those values are of little use in risk adjusting the outcomes.

To perform this assessment we need to:

> Take each implicit and explicit dependency in our Value Stream Map and assess the interfaces between the capabilities and how these drive the capabilities.

> Assign the cost, risk, and operational needs to produce a tangible assessment of the tradeoffs between the needed capabilities.

Step 4   Define Explicit, Balanced, and Feasible Alternatives

For each capability that has been identified and analyzed, a tradeoff assessment of its usefulness to the project using some form of the measure of cost and benefit must be performed. These tradeoffs connect cost, schedule, and technical performance into a single *trade space.*[5] The notion of a trade space provides the means to explore alternatives in design and development early in the project. The tradeoffs are compared to see how well they provide the needed capabilities to the customer. The MoEs and MoPs can be used to assess the alternatives during the trade space analysis.

We must remember that the project's value is realized only when the capabilities the project produces are those needed for success as defined by the users. This is the definition of value used by the agile community. It is a definition that is universal and directly supported by the capabilities-based planning paradigm of Performance-Based Project Management described in Chapter 2.

For the alternatives to be usable, they must:

> ➤ Be monetized in some way to assess the connections between cost, risk, value, and compliance with the technical performance requirements. This "trade space" is part of our decision-making process. What do we need? What can we afford? How much risk can we tolerate? What are the upsides and downsides of accepting this risk?

> ➤ Provide tradeoffs measured in units of effectiveness and performance. These need to be *risk adjusted*. We'll see how to do this in Chapter 5.

Identify the Requirements Baseline

Poorly formed requirements contribute up to 25 percent to the failure of projects.[6] Requirements engineering is the result of requirements elicitation, requirements specification, and requirements validation. Most of the requirements management techniques and tools today focus on a specification—that is, the representation of the requirements. Our Performance-Based Project Management method concentrates instead on elicitation. This method addresses problems found with requirements engineering that are not adequately addressed by specification techniques.[7] Our Five Immutable Practices incorporate advantages of existing elicitation techniques while providing new techniques to elicit requirements. These techniques include fact-finding, requirements gathering, evaluation and rationalization, prioritization, and integration.

Once we know what "done" looks like in Measures of Effectiveness derived from our capabilities, we can start to define the technical and operational requirements that need to be fulfilled to deliver these capabilities. But remember, requirements are not the same as capabilities.

And capabilities are not the same as requirements. Both are needed, but capabilities come first; the requirements follow. Without this sequence, the requirements have no home.

There are five steps to establishing the requirements baseline.

Step 1 Perform Fact-Finding

We start by eliciting information to produce an overall statement of the project's goal in its operational context. This provides the operational and technical objectives to be met by the project and answers two important questions: "What problem does the customer want to solve?" and "How will we recognize that the problem is solved?"

To perform this fact-finding, we need to take these steps:

1. **Identify the relevant parties across multiple levels of the requirements breakdown.** This is done using a list of the project stakeholders, participants, and suppliers assigned to each of the capabilities and the related requirements, and it provides the traceability needed to see who influences the use, consumption, creation, and constraints on the requirements.

2. **Determine the operational and problem context.** This includes the operational modes, goals, and business scenarios. Using the Concept of Operations, we can create a cross-reference between the project's operational behavior and the stakeholders to confirm that they are going to get what they expect to get.

3. **Identify similar systems and elements of these systems to help reveal requirements.** Learning the attributes of similar systems can save us time and reduce risk.

4. **Perform a context analysis for each requirement to isolate redundancy and duplication.** This effort answers the questions, "Why is this requirement here?" "What value does it provide?" and "How can we measure its value?" Evaluating each requirement and how these requirements support the needed capabilities is the start of the economic assessment of the project.

FIGURE 2.3 Work packages define specific activities leading to a capability.

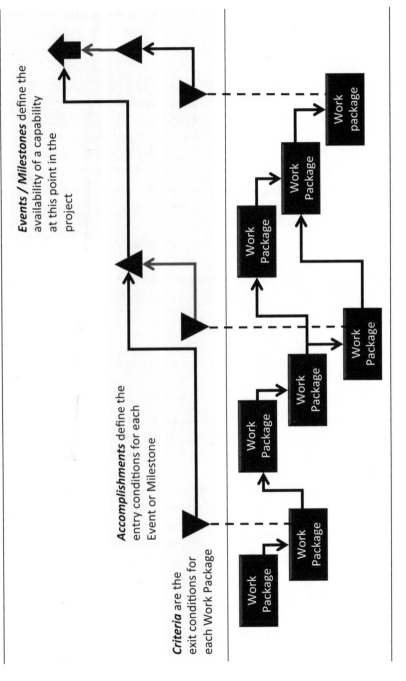

Events / Milestones define the availability of a capability at this point in the project

Accomplishments define the entry conditions for each Event or Milestone

Criteria are the exit conditions for each Work Package

5. **Identify the domain experts we'll need to provide information about the requirements and their connection to the needed capabilities.** Connect these experts to specific capabilities and trace their recommendations to requirements and their prioritization.

6. **Identify the domain and architecture models for each requirement and how these models interact with each other.** This allows us to offer technical options for each requirement. These tradeoffs give us insight into the cost assessment process.

7. **Assess any cost and implementation constraints imposed by the project owner.** Associate these cost tradeoffs with each requirement based on a formal cost structure. This is the start of the value assessment of the project. It is difficult to know what the value of a capability is without knowing its cost.

Step 2   Gather and Classify the Requirements

With our fact-finding complete for each of the elicited requirements, we can now start to classify them. An easy way is to build categories that match the business capabilities. We can gather the operational, technical, functional, nonfunctional, and environmental requirements, along with the design constraints. With these, we can build a top-down list of capabilities and deconstruct the requirements. This is easily done in a "requirements flow-down tree," where the root of the tree is the top-level business goals of the project. Each capability is the child of the root of this tree, and the requirements can then be connected to each needed capability. Making these connections visible is the key to success.

To gather and classify the requirements we need to:

> ➤ Capture a "list" of requirements derived from the ConOps in some form of structured "tree." This allows us to identify the connectivity between the requirements from the very beginning of the project. These connections may not be correct, so we need to continuously improve these structures as the project progresses.

> ➢ Classify these requirements according to their functional, nonfunctional, environment, and design attributes. Partition the assignment of these requirements separately from the capabilities-based requirements. We must avoid the simple "wish list" approach with no means of separating value, risk, cost, feasibility, and other show-stopper attributes.

Step 3 Evaluate and Rationalize the Requirements

We now need to look at each requirement and ask, "Is this something that we really need?" "What happens if this requirement is dropped?" "Who is impacted by this requirement?" We need to define the connections between the requirements of the stakeholder and the beneficial outcomes from the project.

This is done through a cost/benefit assessment of the variables and dependencies:

> ➢ Answer questions such as, "Why do you need Requirement X?" We can use some form of dependency modeling to connect the "need" to the requirement. The traceability from need to requirement is made visible to all participants so they can understand the impact on the cost and schedule for each requirement.

> ➢ Capture the rationale for each requirement. This is done with a narrative explaining how this requirement supports a needed capability.

> ➢ Perform a risk assessment, addressing technical, cost, and schedule concerns once the connections are made. This includes cost/benefit filtering and feasibility analysis based on technology attributes, such as technical performance, reliability, serviceability, or other attributes of the product or service produced by the project. Once we map risks to individual requirements, we get the information needed to manage risks and make tradeoffs based on risk. This activity takes place in the fourth practice.

Step 4 Prioritize the Requirements

Put these requirements in order of priority, starting with the must-haves. If the outcomes can't deliver these requirements, the project is a failure. If they can, these are the requirements to be used in the next step.

This prioritization is straightforward:

> **Determine criticality of the essential functions for the mission.** Build a ranked list of critical elements using a paired-comparison analysis with geometric progression.[8]

> **Sequence requirements based on cost and dependency.** Assess how the system can be incrementally added to, and identify appropriate architectural models that support incremental development. If we build a model of these requirements that connects them to the needed capabilities and to each other, we can assess the impact of each requirement beyond just "making a list."

Step 5 Integrate and Validate the Requirements

Using the ranked requirements, connect them by asking, "What data are needed, who is affected, and what high-level processes will be implemented as a result of this requirement?" Get this right for the ranked requirements before doing anything else. Then repeat this process for the next tier of requirements. The result is a "completeness" test for the requirements. We can validate and come to agreement on what requirements are needed to fulfill the desired capabilities and resolve any conflicts and inconsistencies.

Here's how this can be done:

> Address completeness by filling in as many "to be determined" requirements as possible. Using the "requirements" model, we can assess any missing components and grade the maturity of the requirements model. This approach allows us to make the "maturity" of the requirements visible in tangible form.

> Validate that requirements are in agreement with originally stated capabilities. With the requirements traceability matrix,

we can connect the requirements to the capabilities and ensure that each capability can be fulfilled with an explicitly defined solution.

> Obtain authorization and verification to move to the next step
in the Five Immutable Practices—the development of our Performance Measurement Baseline. Once the requirements are in
place, the scope of the project is defined in preparation for the
planning process.

Establish the Performance
Measurement Baseline

The Performance Measurement Baseline (PMB) is the primary representation of the project's cost, schedule, and technical performance plan.
Constructing the PMB requires knowledge of the capabilities and requirements, skill in developing the work packages (WPs) that produce
the deliverables for these requirements, and discipline to assemble the
cost and schedule relationships between the work packages. This discipline requires greater focus on the part of the project management
staff. Without this discipline, it is simply not possible to develop a credible baseline, and the project is set up for failure because no one knows
what "done" looks like.

The project management staff must know in intimate detail each
WP, its deliverables and resource requirements, the performance measurement criteria, and the dependencies that form the critical path
through the project schedule.

The PMB defines the following:

> Deliverables with units of measure describing progress to plan

> Deliverables that are known to be what the customer is paying
money for

> Deliverables that implement the needed capabilities

The first critical success factor in building the PMB is the deconstruction of the system requirements into technical capabilities, then into deliverables that enable those technical capabilities, and finally into a work breakdown structure and the work packages that produce those deliverables. This is illustrated in Figure 3.2.

The physical construction of the WPs takes many forms, based on the needs of the project. Their format is not critical. The contents are. The format of the WPs should be appropriate to the needs of the project.

The Principle of Performance-Based Project Management using WPs requires that we:

> ➤ Define the deliverables independent of the needed system capabilities in a work breakdown structure. This deconstruction process MUST be iterative and incremental. Assessment of its reliability and deconstruction requires thought. The first deconstruction is likely not the best approach.

> ➤ Estimate the duration and work effort for each WP. Estimating duration and effort is also iterative and incremental; it cannot be a one-time effort. The initial estimate MUST be assessed after the assembly of the WPs into the Activity Network of the tasks performing the work. Only then can they be considered credible.

There are six steps in doing this work, but the approach here is to define the work in packages—small chunks of effort that produce a tangible outcome. This outcome goes toward fulfilling a requirement, which, in turn, enables a capability. By now, you should be seeing a pattern—little steps.[9]

This, of course, is similar to agile development—do a little, test it, do a little more. This is the basis of Performance-Based Project Management. Build the project performance management system in little steps. This is not a new approach. It is a logical approach. But often this approach is not used. Instead, the big bang approach is used. Define all the work, build a huge and convoluted schedule, and start executing that schedule. This is a really bad idea and usually leads to project failure, because what "done" looks like hasn't been defined, and, therefore, how is progress toward "done" going to be measured along the way, other than through the passage of time and consumption of money?

Step 1   Deconstruct the Project Scope
into Work Packages

This starts with building a work breakdown structure showing the products and the processes needed to produce those products. The WBS is always "product centric," not functional. The WBS shows what is going to be delivered, so we can trace the deliverables back to the requirements and then back to the needed capabilities.

Figure 3.2 shows how to:

> ➤ **Use the WBS to define the work packages that need to be scheduled and staffed.** Resources and functions need to be assigned to each of the work packages.

> ➤ **Deconstruct the requirements into collections of deliverables at the terminal nodes of the WBS.** "Lumps of work" can be assembled for assignment to the subject-matter experts, who can then estimate the cost and schedule. Discovering how these "lumps of work" are related is an iterative and incremental process, so plan on doing this several times.

> ➤ **Revisit the necessity for each requirement and the work needed to fulfill the capability.** Trace each requirement back to its source capability to make sure we have a reason for the requirement and the requirement supports a needed capability. Without this final connection check we may end up with unneeded requirements or unfulfilled capabilities.

Step 2   Assign Responsibility for the Delivery
of These Work Packages

After defining the work packages, the resources need to be assigned. The easiest way to do this is with a Responsibility Assignment Matrix (RAM). The RAM identifies the person accountable for each work package. Assigning accountability is mandatory. The person accountable can then assign responsibility to others doing the related work. This single point of integrative responsibility removes the confusion over who has the information about the performance of the work package and who is accountable for it.

Step 3 Arrange the Work Packages in a Logical Order

This is where the heavy lifting on any project starts. We need to arrange the work packages in a well-formed network with explicitly defined deliverables, milestones, and internal and external dependencies. The schedule that results from this sequencing effort describes the delivery of products or services, shows dependencies, shows deliverables, shows how maturity increases, identifies risks and their mitigation or retirement, and provides other measures meaningful to project management and the stakeholders.

Step 4 Assign Resources and Costs to
These Work Packages

We start with a budget for each work package. This can be labor hour "spreads" and material costs. This *cost spread* can be made visible with a scheduling tool. This will be important when we start measuring the performance of our project. There are several ways to come up with the "estimated budget." The best is to use past performance: "What did it take to develop a similar product or service in the past?" If we don't have that identical information directly, we can use a *reference class forecast*. Reference class forecasting predicts the outcome of a planned action based on actual outcomes in a reference class of similar actions to that being forecast. The theories behind reference class forecasting were developed by Daniel Kahneman and Amos Tversky.[10]

Step 5 Assign Measures of Physical Percent Complete to Each Outcome

We can now assign objective performance measures for each work package and summarize these at the project level. These objective measures are assigned to deliverables in units meaningful to the decision makers. This measure of physical percent complete (PPC) is an unequivocal assessment of progress. It "shows" results through tangible evidence, never opinion, or measures of effort, passage of time, or consumption of resources.

The best way to measure physical progress to plan is to use a 0 percent/100 percent assessment of "done." Either it is "done" or it is not "done"—nothing in between. The key here is to make fine-grained measures for planned work. One way to do this is to ask yourself, "How long are you willing to wait before you find out you are late?" Then define the assessment of physical percent complete at one-half that duration. That way, when you learn you are going to be late, there is time to fix it and get back on plan.

Step 6 Set the Performance Measurement Baseline

With the first five steps in place, we're now ready to "baseline" our plan. We have identified all the capabilities, resolved all the requirements, and assigned them to the needed capabilities. We built a work breakdown structure from these requirements and connected these to the work packages. We sequenced the work packages, resource loading them, and assigning single accountabilities for the deliverables from the work packages. This prepares us to set the Performance Measurement Baseline. The PMB is a budgeted plan for all the work to be performed, the organizations needed to perform that work, the descriptions of the outcomes, and measures of these outcomes.

FIGURE 3.2 Performance Measurement Baseline.

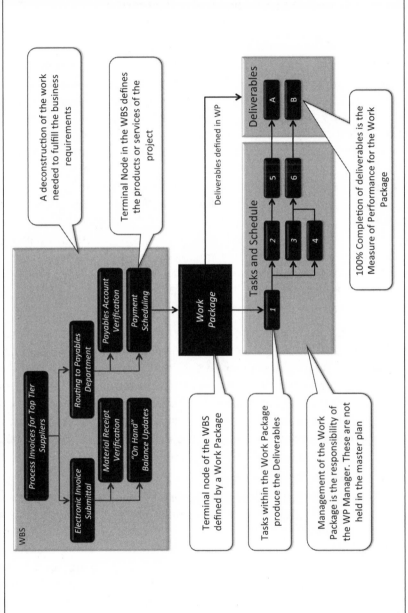

Execute the Performance Measurement Baseline

Using the Performance Measurement Baseline, each work package must start as planned, complete on or near the planned date, and produce at or near the planned technical performance level. This is essential to the success of any credible Performance-Based Project Management method. In the absence of this, the project is behind schedule, over budget, and noncompliant with the technical goals. Notice the "on/at or near" phrase. All measures, all work, all plans must contain a margin for naturally occurring variances. They must also have a management reserve for the probabilistic uncertainties that occur on all projects.

The primary focus of the Performance Measurement Baseline execution is to physically assess the progress of the project in units reflecting three independent variables. All these variables are probabilistic, with confidence intervals. These means we must speak about a cost or a schedule date or a technical performance using our "at or below" for cost, "on or before" for a date, and "within tolerance" for a technical performance. And then use them with some confidence.

> **Cost.** This is the budgeted and actual cost for all labor and materials used in the project. We determine our budget performance by comparing our planned spending with the actual spending on a time-phased basis. The assessment does not tell us about actual progress of course, just how we are spending money toward that progress. We must speak about cost as, "We have an 80 percent confidence that the project's cost will be $1,225,500 or less on the planned completion date."

> **Schedule.** This is the sequenced set of work activities needed to deliver the outcomes of the project. We can measure progress to our schedule by looking at how we start and end the work packages. The assessment of "late starts" and "late finishes" is a good indicator of project performance. We'll use this information in Chapter 5 to construct an "Estimate to Complete" for our sample project. We must speak about the schedule date as, "We have an 80 percent confidence of completion on or before September 30, 2014."

> **Technical Performance.** This is the assessment of the outcomes against the planned performance needed to satisfy the needed capabilities. This is the best measure of project performance. Cost and schedule are necessary, but, in the end, the product or service must actually work as planned. We predefine the expected "technical performance" of the outcomes of the work packages and assess their measures at the planned time. We must speak about technical performance as, "We have an 85 percent confidence that the system can process 10,000 transactions an hour in the first month of operation and increase to 15,000 transactions an hour after full operational checkout."

The comparison of budget versus actual expenditures indicates what was planned to be spent versus what was actually spent at any given time. The comparison of actual technical performance with planned technical performance indicates how we are meeting the requirements and the resulting capabilities. We must be "on budget, on schedule, and on specification" for our project's probability of success to increase.

With this approach, the use of physical percent complete for the amount of work performed is a starting point. It does not indicate anything about the conformance to specification of the work produced for the amount of money spent.

To successfully execute the PMB, we need to take five steps.

Step 1 Perform the Work in the Planned Order

Apply a Work Authorization process for starting work packages. The authorization process defines the planned start, actual start, projected finish, and actual finish. This makes our performance visible for all authorized work in the coming period of performance and confirms readiness to perform the work against our allocated budget. A fundamental rule of project management is "late start = late finish." Keeping track of "late starts" and "late finishes" provides visibility to the project ability to meet its commitments.

Step 2 Capture and Report the Performance of the Work

Using measures of physical percent complete, the actual cost of the work is captured and compared to the budgeted cost. These actual costs are important to forecast future costs, but they are not measures of actual progress. To measure actual progress, we need both schedule performance and technical performance.

When we capture measures of physical percent complete, we must define what we expect it "should" be on the day we take this measure. The best measure of physical percent assessments is a "working product." This means working software, working hardware, and a working process.

Step 3 Analyze the Performance

Analysis of the project's performance takes many forms. Some are subjective, many objective. Let's focus on the objective assessments of performance for now:

> **The Critical Path.** This is the longest path through the network of activities. If this path were to get "longer," the project would slip. But there are "near critical" paths as well. These paths are the source of most of the scheduling problems. When a "near critical" path becomes a critical path, it is usually too late to take corrective actions.

> **Duration Accuracy.** This must be realistic and risk adjusted. Having a measure of variance for duration, cost, and technical performance provides credibility to the project's schedule. We must remember that all project variables are random numbers. Knowing the value of a number is necessary but not sufficient. We must also know the variance of any number for that number to be credible for use in managing the project.

> **Integration.** All the work packages must be connected horizontally as well as vertically. Horizontal connections are the sequence within a work stream, the intradependencies. Vertical

integration describes the interdependencies between the work that produces increasing value to the project through the delivered capabilities.

> **Reality Testing.** This is needed if we are to actually achieve the desired results. It starts with a "risk adjusted" cost and schedule baseline.

> **Forecasting.** This is the prediction of the future cost, schedule, and technical performance based on past performance and risk management.

Step 4 Take Corrective Actions to Keep the Planned Work Moving Forward

With the cost, schedule, and technical performance indices we can construct a forecast of future performance of cost, schedule, and technical performance compliance efforts, and take management actions for any work packages not performing as planned by doing the following:

> Calculating measured performance using tangible evidence of physical percent complete

> Recording changes to the work sequencing, scope, budget, or any other variable and agreeing these changes will not negatively impact the outcome of the project without agreement from the stakeholders

> Adjusting the sequence of work, budget, or resources to correct the undesirable outcomes of the current performance of the project

Step 5 Maintain the Integrity of the Performance Measurement Baseline

When we record past performance based on work package completion criteria, we can construct and estimate the future forecast. We can then manage the schedule, the labor, and other cost spreads through the performance measures of the deliverables using a change-controlled baseline. We capture the data from each period of performance and add that information to the PMB to record past performance, which we can use for future performance forecasts. These data of past, present, and future performance measures ensure that we have visibility into the project for management, technical experts, and project, planning, and controls staff.

Perform Continuous Risk Management

While we are off executing the Performance Measurement Baseline, we need to be mindful that project management is actually about the continuous management of risk. The notion of Continuous Risk Management (number 5 in Figure 3.1) is critical to the success of using Performance-Based Project Management. Risk management is not a one-time activity; it is performed "continuously" at every step along the way. The identification and management of risk is performed throughout project management.

The six steps to Continuous Risk Management are shown in Figure 3.3.[11]

Step 1 Identify Risks

Before risks can be managed, they must be identified. Identification surfaces risks before they become problems and adversely affect a project. The Software Engineering Institute (SEI) has developed techniques for surfacing risks by using a disciplined and systematic process that encourages project personnel to raise concerns and issues for subsequent analysis.

To identify risks we must:

> ➤ Capture a statement of risk describing the name of the risk, the probability of the risk occurring, the potential impact of the risk if it were to occur, and risk handling plans to either retire the risk or handle the risk if it were to occur.

> ➤ Capture the context of a risk that provides additional information about the circumstances of the risk.[12] The context is a detailed description of the events, circumstances, and interrelationships that may affect the project.

Step 2   Analyze the Risks

The analysis then converts this risk data into risk decision-making information. This information guides the project manager to work on the "right" risks. This analysis examines the risks in detail to determine the extent of the risks, how they relate to each other, and which risks are the most important.

To analyze risk, we need to do the following:

> ➤ Evaluate the attributes of the risks to gain a better understanding of the risk to determine the expected impact, probability, and time frame of the risk.

> ➤ Classify the risks by looking at the set of risks and how the risks relate to each other as a class. The classes or groups of risk provide different perspectives when planning the risk-mitigation processes.

> ➤ Prioritize and rank the risks to separate which risks should be dealt with and in what order when allocating resources.

Step 3   Plan the Risk-Handling Strategies

Risk planning turns risk analysis information into decisions and necessary present and future actions to handle the risk. Planning develops actions to address individual risks, prioritize the actions, and create an integrated Risk Management Plan. This planning effort helps managers decide what if anything should be done with the risk. Planning produces risk action plans for individual or classes of risks. Risks are planned by the people who have the knowledge, expertise, background, and resources to effectively deal with the risks.

This planning process needs to:

> Assign responsibility, starting with a review of the project risks by the project manager to determine what to do with them. This ensures that no risk is ignored.

> Define the approach for handling the risk. This starts with knowing enough about the risk to decide what to do, and then picking an appropriate approach for management of the risk.

> Define the scope and actions needed for a balanced approach in developing effective handling actions to mitigate risks.

Step 4 Track the Status of the Risk-Handling Strategies

Tracking monitors the status of risks and the actions taken to ameliorate them. Appropriate risk metrics are identified and monitored to evaluate the status of the risks and of risk mitigation plans. Tracking serves as the "watchdog" function of management. The person responsible for the tracking process:

> Acquires information about the risk by collecting data about the context, impact, probability, time frame, rank, and planned approach for each risk.

> Compiles which data for a given risk are analyzed, combined, calculated, and organized for tracking the risk and the risk-handling plans.

> Reports this tracking information in a Risk Management Plan (RMP) used to communicate risk status and handling plans. These reports are delivered as part of routine project management activities of the project.

Step 5　Control the Risk-Handling Activities

The decision-making process takes the tracking status reports produced in the fourth step and decides what to do with the risks. The person accountable for a risk normally makes the control decisions for that risk.

Step 6　Communicate the Risk Information

Risk communication is at the center of all successful risk management processes. Without effective communication, no risk management approach is viable. To be analyzed and managed correctly, risks must be communicated to and among the appropriate organizational levels and entities. This includes levels within the project organization, the customer organization, and, most especially, across the interfaces between the project and customer. Because communication is pervasive, this approach is integral to every risk management activity and is not something performed outside of, and as a supplement to, other activities.

FIGURE 3.3 Communication is at the center of Continuous Risk Management.

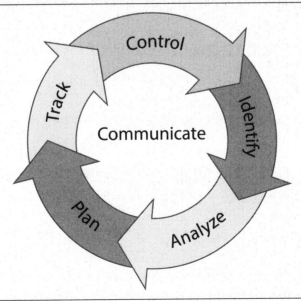

Looking Back

We now have Five Practices to go with our Five Immutable Principles. Figure 3.4 shows these connections. The Five Principles are connected to the Five Practices through the components of project management.

> ➤ The Concept of Operations (ConOps) is the narrative of what capabilities the project will need to deliver for the stakeholder to consider the project a success.

> ➤ The technical and operational requirements define how the capabilities will be fulfilled.

> ➤ The master schedule shows how the work packages deliver the requirements at the planned time and for the planned cost.

> ➤ The work packages contain the activities needed to produce the outcomes that meet the project's planned performance objectives.

> ➤ Measures of physical percent complete ensure that progress is being made to plan.

> ➤ Continuous Risk Management processes are performed on all activities of the project.

What's Ahead?

With the principles and practices in place, we now need a process framework we can use to apply them before moving to our project examples. This framework is necessary to anchor our principles and practices in the "governance" process. Governance is the management framework for making decisions about the project. The accountabilities and responsibilities associated with the business processes are defined by governance.

This process framework is based on five guidelines:

1. **Organizing.** People perform projects. Organizing people to perform the work is a critical success factor for all projects.

FIGURE 3.4 The Five Immutable Principles and Five Immutable Practices are connected.

5 Immutable Practices of Project Success	5 Immutable Principles of Project Success				
	Capabilities Baseline	Requirements Baseline	Performance Measurement Baseline	PMB Execution	Continuous Risk Management
1 What does "done" look like?	Concept of Operations	Technical and Operational Requirements			Identify Risks
2 How can we get to "done"?			Master Schedule		Analyze Risks
3 Do we have all the resources we need?			Work Package Sequencing	Work Authorization	Measure Risks
4 What are the impediments to reaching "done"?			Master Schedule	Physical Percent Complete	Monitor Risks
5 How can we measure progress toward "done"?			Master Schedule	Master Schedule	Retire Risks

2. **Planning and Budgeting.** The plan is the strategy for the successful completion of a project. This strategy is a hypothesis of how we will execute the project. We must test this hypothesis while performing the work by measuring outcomes to see if they are technically compliant with our plan. If not, we need to take corrective action and adjust our plan.

3. **Accounting.** We need to keep track of our budget and compare how we are spending the budget to our plan.

4. **Performance Analysis.** Measuring progress to plan allows us to not only make adjustments but also to forecast future performance of the project.

5. **Revision Management and Corrective Actions.** All project work has cost variance, schedule variance, and technical variance. We must manage the project in the presence of these variances. Feedback from the project provides us the information we need to manage in the presence of these variances.

CHAPTER 4

The Five Governing Processes of Project Management

With the Five Principles and Five Practices under our belts, we are almost ready to start managing projects. First, we need the process management framework to help us apply these principles and practices. To be useful, this framework has to be *general purpose*; that is, it must be applicable to any type of project in any domain. We approach this process framework through project governance,[1] which is the mechanism that defines the decision rights for the project and determines how those decisions are made using the principles and practices. Decision rights set the "rules" for how choices pertaining to planning, developing, and executing the project are made by the project's participants. Once the project is initiated, capabilities, requirements, planning, budget, control, and management all create situations in which someone has to decide. The decision rights process is the mechanism for making those decisions. In the absence of decision rights, the project participants have few mechanisms for resolving the conflicts that normally arise.

Project governance is concerned with five areas: Business success, customer impact, team impact, project efficiency, and preparation for the future[2] are critical factors in the success of all projects. While the principles and practices are necessary for project success, we also need processes to guide us in how to apply them. Governance tells us what processes, principles, and practices are needed and how they are to be implemented within a process framework. Project governance tells us how to make decisions, including how to decide what capabilities are needed at the start of the project. These decisions also tell us how to determine what requirements are appropriate for fulfilling the needed business capabilities, how to ascertain which risks are applicable to what parts of the project and how to handle these risks, and in what order the functionality of the project should be delivered to meet the business needs. Project governance fills the gap between the business users, who are the recipients, and the producers, who are the creators, of the project's capabilities and requirements.[3]

Implementing the Five Processes

In traditional project management, the white space between the project's technology development activities and the project's business processes, which use this technology, is often missing. This white space exists only when gaps are created between the project mission, the strategy that fulfills this mission, the project execution, and the project's delivery of value to the stakeholders. When there is white space in the project, there is no clear connection between the mission of the project and the technical or operational solutions that are supposed to deliver value to the business. There is no "line of sight" visibility from the need to the solution. When this happens, the gaps are many times filled in by unneeded or even undesired features.

Alignment gaps appear when business investments in the project are not traceable to the business strategy. An alignment gap appears when there is no connection between behavior of the system and the business policies that guide the system. The users of the system don't know "why" they are doing what they are doing. To close these gaps and deliver the business capabilities we need to identify what "done" looks like. *Execution* gaps appear when those tasked with delivering products and services do not have a clear "line of sight" to the business strategy. To close these gaps, we need to identify the needed capabilities, the technical and operational requirements, the Performance Measurement Baseline, and the risk-handling strategies we are going to apply to the project. In other words, the gaps are closed using the principles, practices, and processes of Performance-Based Project Management, which are illustrated in Figure 4.1.

As project managers, we are technocrats managing the construction of products or the delivery of services. Our connection to the business world usually "flows down" through documents in the form of specifications or Statements of Work. If we think of the Five Principles and Five Practices as the bricks and mortar of the project, it becomes obvious that we need one more thing before we can proceed. Using our principles and practices, we need a set of rules to guide the project architecture—these rules are called governance,[4] and they apply to five areas: business success, customer impact, team impact, project efficiency, and preparation for the future. Together, they connect the principles, practices, and processes. Their relationship is illustrated in Figure 4.2. We will not further discuss the governance areas here, because they are outside the domain of this book, but we will use them to tie the principles, practices, and processes together to form the basis of Performance-Based Project Management.[5]

FIGURE 4.1 The gaps between each process.

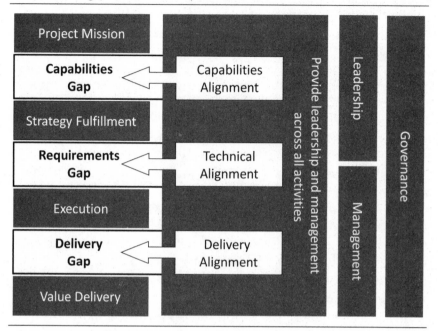

FIGURE 4.2 Governance, principles, practices, and processes are required for success.

	Governance	Principles	Practices	Processes
1	Business success	What does "done" look like?	Identify capabilities	Organize the project
2	Customer impact	How do we get to "done?"	Identify baseline requirements	Plan, schedule, and budget
3	Team impact	Do we have enough resources?	Develop Performance Measurement Baseline	Execute project accounting
4	Project efficiency	What are the impediments to progress?	Execute Performance Measurement Baseline	Execute project performance analysis
5	Preparation for the future	How do we measure progress?	Implement Continuous Risk Management	Revise and maintain data

Deploying the Five Processes

We are now ready to implement the five processes needed to increase the probability of project success:

1. **Organize the project.** Define the work, determine who is going to do the work, and document these in some manner for others to see. The result is a work breakdown structure (WBS) and an organizational breakdown structure (OBS), which describe the relationships among the participants in the project—the engineers, managers, and supervisors—and the roles they play on the project. The OBS is the "roster" of participants on the project and their individual capabilities. The intersection of the WBS and OBS defines the person accountable for delivering project outcomes. This can be a single individual or several individuals, accountable to each other and to the project manager.

2. **Plan, schedule, and budget.** Plan the order of the deliverables for the project, schedule the work needed to produce those deliverables, and develop the budget for the work. These three items are the least amount of information needed to manage the project. Anything less lowers the probability of project success.

3. **Execute project accounting.** Capture the actual costs of doing the planned work and compare these costs to the budgeted costs. This information and the measures of physical percent complete are used to assess the performance of the project and identify corrective actions needed to keep on schedule, on budget, and in technical compliance with the planned outcomes that provide the needed capabilities for the customer, while the technical and operational requirements are being implemented.

4. **Execute project performance analysis.** With the project plan and the actual work on the project, we can now assess cost and schedule performance and technical outcomes. This analysis allows us to determine variances, so that we can take corrective action to keep the project going as planned.

5. **Record revisions and maintain data.** When there are changes to cost, schedule, capabilities, and technical performance requirements, we must record these changes so we don't forget what changes we made and why we made them.

With these five processes we can assemble a project management method that will increase the probability of success of projects in a wide variety of business and technical domains.

Organize the Project

"Projects are performed by people, constrained by limited resources and have to be planned, executed, and controlled."[6] Projects are executed by people, against a plan for the work to be performed, to produce outcomes implemented by the deliverables, using the tools and processes to manage and control the project outcomes. We need to know how the elements of the project are organized. Who's in charge? Who is assigned to what work? What resources are available to the project for performing the work? What skills are needed to perform this work? What is being produced by these work efforts? How these products or services related to each other? All these questions are answered using the organizing processes that follow.

For project success, the participants need a mutual understanding of the answers to each of these questions. The answer to, "What are we delivering to the customer?" is provided by the work breakdown structure. The answer to, "Who is doing the work that delivers the outcomes from each element of the WBS?" is provided by the organizational breakdown structure. Figure 4.3 illustrates what the answers to the "what" questions for a hypothetical kitchen renovation might be. The answers to the "who" questions for this renovation are contained in the OBS section of Figure 4.4. We will use this WBS and OBS, along with the intersections that create the work packages, in the coming chapters, along with other examples, to show how to apply the principles, practices, and processes.

FIGURE 4.3 Work breakdown structure for kitchen renovation.

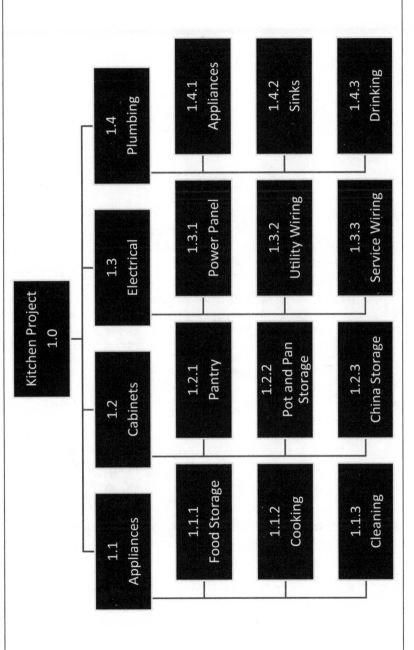

FIGURE 4.4 People do the work that delivers the outcomes.

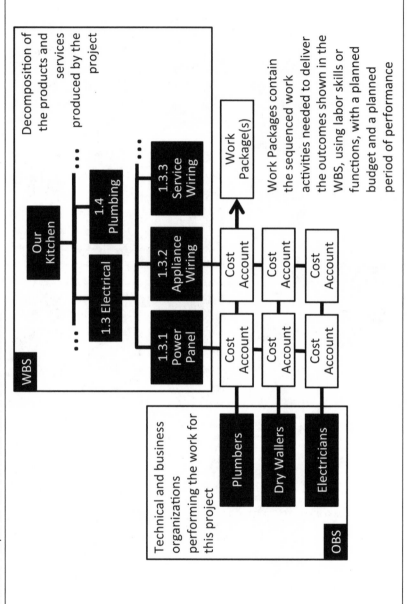

Define the Deliverable Outcomes

All work breakdown structures are not alike.[7] It can be a formal WBS, such as those found in construction[8] and defense programs.[9] Or it can be a less formal deconstruction of the work by simply listing the outcomes of the project on a white board in your office. The *PMBOK® Guide* says the WBS is "a deliverable-oriented hierarchical deconstruction of the work to be executed by the project team to accomplish the project objectives and create the required deliverables."[10] In the agile paradigm, each user story represents work that produces a deconstruction. Like formal approaches to the WBS, Agile organizes project outcomes around features and functions that result from the work efforts. No matter the domain, complexity of the problem, or the method for developing products, some type of deconstruction of the deliverables is mandatory. Without this deconstruction, there is no way to determine what is to be built, who is supposed to build it, and what "done" looks like.

The WBS is the foundation for initiating, planning, executing, monitoring, and controlling the work to produce the desired outcomes of the project. It is the representation of the work scope of the project, documenting the hierarchy and describing the deliverables to be produced by the work efforts and their relationships to the final outcome of the project. It "breaks down" all the work into deliverable elements for planning, budgeting, scheduling, cost accounting, work authorization, measuring progress, and management control. This sounds like a lot of work, but if we are going to determine the project's final cost and schedule, we need to know what it is we are supposed to be delivering. We can then develop the WBS dictionary—the narrative description of the deliverables, their defined outcomes, and their units of measure for success—to define the work scope for each unique element in the WBS.

Identify the Resources Performing the Work

With the defined work shown in the WBS, we can now assign the organizational responsibility for this work. An OBS does this. The organizational breakdown structure shows the responsibility, accountability, and authority for all tasks to be performed. It is a direct representation of the organizational hierarchy and describes the organizational elements that provide resources, plan, and perform the work. It identifies the organization responsible for each segment of work, including subcontracted and intraorganizational efforts. The assignment of lower-level work segments to responsible managers provides key control points for managing the project. When effort is subcontracted, the applicable subcontractor is identified and related to the appropriate WBS element(s) or organization accountable for acquiring the subcontracted item.

Integrate the Work with the Resources Performing the Work

Integrating the WBS and OBS creates connections between the resources doing the work and the work itself; this is illustrated in Figure 4.4. The "intersection" of WBS and OBS is where we assign the budget needed to do the work and collect costs for the labor and materials needed to produce the project's outcome. It is the point where a single functional organization or integrated product team has responsibility for work that delivers to a single WBS element. This intersection is called a *control account*. It is also where we examine the status of our work efforts. This process is always focused on physical percent complete, rather than on simple cost and schedule reporting. Progress toward "done" is the primary measure of success.

A Checklist for Organizing the Project

A checklist is vital to any project; it ensures that we don't forget anything along the way. Here are some questions that need answers before we move on:

> ➤ Does the WBS contain all the project work? If the planned work is not in the WBS, why are we doing it? If we are doing it, where can I find the work in the WBS and the WBS dictionary?

> ➤ If we are subcontracting any of the work, is that work in the WBS as well? When we say "all in," it means all the work, not just the work we want to do.

> Is there a target budget for all of the work? Has this budget been developed bottom up by resources accountable for the work? Top-down budgets may be easy to do, but they lay the groundwork for project failure. Only after the bottom-up budget is developed can the project manager and business management have something to say about it. If the budget is flowed down from the top, then the bottom-up estimate needs to confirm the credibility of the budget.

> Are all the elements of work in the WBS assigned to the proper organizations or resources? We need to know "who is doing what" so there is no overlap or gap in our resource plan.

> Do we know the total target budget for this project? With the complete list of deliverables, do we know all the work needed to produce those deliverables and the estimated budget for that work?

> Do we know who is accountable for the budgets, the technical, and the managerial aspects of the project? This list is represented in the OBS (see Figure 4.4).

> Is there a single person accountable for each deliverable? Collective accountability lays the groundwork for project difficulties. Without a single voice for "progress to plan," business management gets confused.

Plan, Schedule, and Budget the Project

For every project, no matter the domain, we need to plan, schedule, and budget for the work. This seems like an obvious set of activities, a tautology. But there are many times when the "proper" planning, scheduling, and budgeting don't happen and the project is set on the wrong course from day one. Let's look at the details for how to do this right the first time.

Plan the Work

Planning is not the same as scheduling. Most projects start with scheduling and fail to plan. The plan tells us where we are going. It tells us when our capabilities are needed and in what order they are needed. Figure 4.5 shows the relationship between the plan and the schedule. The plan is a strategy for accomplishing some outcome. It describes where we are going, the various paths we can take to reach our destination, and the performance assessment points along the way to ensure that we are on the right path. These assessment points measure the "maturity" of the product or service against the planned maturity. This is the only real measure of progress. Progress is not measured by the passage of time or the consumption of money. Figure 4.5 illustrates the relationship between the project plan and project schedule and the work packages, which produce the outcomes that deliver accomplishments that meet criteria toward milestones, which measure physical percent complete.

As you can see, the plan and the schedule are not the same thing and must be looked at separately. The plan is a procedure used to achieve an objective. It is a set of intended actions through which one expects to achieve a goal. The schedule is the sequence of the intended actions needed to implement the plan. The plan is the strategy for the successful completion of the project. In the strategic planning domain, a plan is a hypothesis that needs to be tested along the way to confirm where we're headed.[11] The schedule is the order in which the work required to execute the plan will be performed. We need both. Plans without schedules are not executable. Schedules without plans have no stated mission, vision, or description of success other than the execution of the work.

The elements in Figure 4.5 are used to construct the plan and schedule for the delivery of the outcomes of the project. These elements are connected in a single document as the Performance Measurement Baseline, which is used by the project manager:

> ➤ **The milestones show the availability of one or more capabilities.** We showed how to develop these capabilities in Chapter 3. This is where we put them in the proper order for delivering business value to the customer. The name of the milestone in the plan represents its capability. Figure 2.2 is an example of the increasing capabilities provided by a project for the customer.

FIGURE 4.5 Relationship between the project plan and schedule.

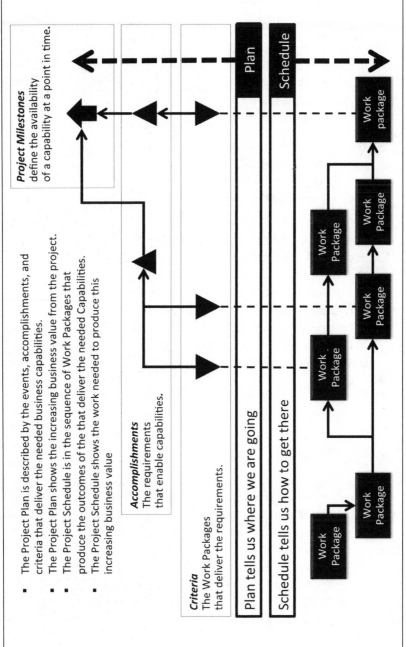

- The Project Plan is described by the events, accomplishments, and criteria that deliver the needed business capabilities.
- The Project Plan shows the increasing business value from the project.
- The Project Schedule is in the sequence of Work Packages that produce the outcomes of the that deliver the needed Capabilities.
- The Project Schedule shows the work needed to produce this increasing business value

Project Milestones
define the availability
of a capability at a point in time.

Accomplishments
The requirements
that enable capabilities.

Criteria
The Work Packages
that deliver the requirements.

Plan tells us where we are going

Schedule tells us how to get there

Plan

Schedule

Work package

Work Package

Work Package

Work Package

Work Package

Work Package

> **The accomplishments and the acceptance criteria for these accomplishments are needed for each of the capabilities delivered to the customer that generates business value.** To measure this value, we need to know what accomplishments must be delivered by the project to produce the capability. For each accomplishment, we need to know its measurement criteria. "How will we recognize that the accomplishment is meeting its goal?"

> **The accomplishments are preconditions that must be met before the capability is ready to deliver its value.** When all the accomplishments are complete and confirmed by their criteria, then the capability is ready to provide value to the customer.

> **The performance of the work activities is always measured in units of physical percent complete.** These activities include those inside the work packages, criteria, accomplishments, and milestones representing the capabilities. We can answer the question, "Where are we in the project?" with a description of what accomplishments have been completed, using the criteria as the measure of physical percent complete against the date for the planned capability being ready to provide business value.

Schedule the Work

Work must be performed in the proper sequence for the technical and business value to be produced by our project. This is demonstrated in Figure 4.5. Defining the right sequence is a "scheduling" activity. No matter what project domain we are working in, doing the right work in the right order is a requirement for success. Imagine what would happen if we install the wallboard in our home and then start to install the electrical wiring. That would be nonsense. The same thing can occur on an IT project or a landscaping project, or any project. The order of work is described in a schedule, with resources and the cost of those resources assigned.

The schedule elements shown in Figure 4.5 are referred to as work packages.

> ➤ Work packages represent units of work at the level where the work is performed. They collect the work tasks into a single "package of work" with a single output from that work.

> ➤ Their implementation is assignable to a single organization. The work package manager is accountable for the outcomes from the work effort.

> ➤ They have a scheduled start and finish date and they produce a tangible outcome. The activities within the work package are not dependent on any external connections. No partially completed work can be a predecessor to another work package.

> ➤ They have budget assigned to them for the performance of the work.

> ➤ Their duration is limited to a short span of time, which reduces the risk of discovering that the work effort is late and there is no time to take corrective action.

Budget the Work

The assignment of budget to scheduled work results in a "spend plan" for the project. This "spend plan" and the work that is budgeted is the PMB. The creation, maintenance, and use of the PMB are critical for effective project performance management. The PMB connects the planned work with the budget needed to produce the work, so those funding the work can see not only how much it is going to cost but also how much money will be needed at a specific time—this is the cash demand for the project.

A Checklist for Planning, Scheduling, and Budgeting

Planning, scheduling, and budgeting the work have to take place in a specific order. First, we need a plan showing how the deliverables are going to be developed and what the measures of their progress will be.

The schedule for actually doing the work comes next. With these two in place, we can determine the budget needed for the labor and materials. Here are some questions to ask yourself as you do this:

> ➤ Does our plan (see the upper half of Figure 4.5) describe the order of the accomplishments that deliver the capabilities needed by the customer?

> ➤ Does our schedule (see lower half of Figure 4.5) describe the order of the work packages required to complete the criteria needed to produce the accomplishments?

> ➤ Does this schedule define the duration of the work activities inside work packages in some risk-adjusted way? Schedules without duration margin are late before they start. Nothing ever goes as planned, so building in margin is needed for the schedule to be credible.

> ➤ Does the schedule have hard dates forced on the project by management? If so, the project is late before it starts.

> ➤ Are significant decision points, constraints, and interfaces to the internal and external activities defined in the schedule? Like the WBS, the schedule must be an "all-in" representation of the project.

> ➤ Can we measure "physical percent complete" for each work package and status the schedule with this information to show our actual progress to plan? Without tangible evidence of progress, the schedule is just a "notional picture" and adds very little to the success of the project.

> ➤ Are there meaningful indicators for measures of schedule progress? The passage of time and consumption of resources are not meaningful. Only the production of tangible outcomes that meet the requirements is meaningful.

> ➤ Is there a time-phased budget for the scheduled work? Does this budget include labor as well as materials and other direct costs so the project's management can determine what the overall funding needs are? Are these time-phased budgets assigned to the organizational elements of the project so they can flow the budget down to the resources performing the work?

> ➤ Have we planned our project in discrete, short-duration work packages?

Execute Project Accounting

Someone has to keep track of the money, especially if it is not our own money. No matter if it is our money or someone else's money, knowing how much money we need, how much money we have now, and how much money we have spent so far is important to everyone on the project. All projects require money for labor and materials. Project accounting is responsible for identifying how much money will be needed, how that money is being spent, who is spending it, and how much money will be needed to complete the project. Other costs to the project are usually considered "indirects," and generally they are not in the purview of project management but are part of the larger business management process. These indirects include "overhead," "benefits," "fringe." These are all costs not directly related to producing the outcomes from the project, but they must be in place for the project to be successful.

We can't keep track of the money in any meaningful way until we have some knowledge of how much money we are going to need. No matter the domain or context, accounting for cost starts with the WBS. If we are managing the "functions" inside a project instead of the products, we can use the functional organization—the OBS—to account for the money. In this chapter, we are managing the development and delivery of "products" or "services," so we will focus on the work breakdown structure. The WBS section of Figure 4.4 is derived from the current military standard for building the WBS, MIL-STD-881C. This sounds a bit heavyweight, but this "standard" includes examples for hardware as well as software and is a good starting point for what a "credible" WBS looks like.

Capture Project Costs

With our time-phased "spend plan" shown in Figure 3.2 (Performance Measurement Baseline), we can collect the direct costs using the accounting system consistent with the way the work is budgeted. The allocation of costs is guided by the lowest level of the WBS in Figure 4.4; for example, 1.3.1, the Power Panel. These costs include the direct labor, materials, and other direct costs (ODC) such as travel, equipment in support of the project, engineering, special tooling, and packaging. These are *direct costs* to the project so they need to be to be budgeted and later captured.

We can now determine our actual costs versus our planned costs. This does not tell us about the *value* that was produced by expending these costs for the work effort. That has to be done by measuring the physical percent complete produced by the work effort. We measure the project's progress against our budget using some simple ideas:

> ➤ The value that we are earning equals our budget multiplied by the physical percent complete at the time of the measurement. This is the literal definition of *earned value* in a more formal domain. It is also a useful measure for any project performance assessment. The question that needs to be answered is, "What value did I get from my investment (budget)?"

> ➤ We can ask and answer a simple question to make this clear: "If we invested $100, did we get $100 of value back on the day we planned to get it back?" The question can be asked for project work, too: "Did we complete the work for the planned budget using the 100 percent complete criteria?" In other words, is the work 100 percent "done"? If it is, we "earned" our budgeted cost. If not, we only "earned" a portion of the budgeted cost and are likely behind schedule and over budget, because we have more work to do and someone has to pay for that work.

Summarize All the Costs by Elements of Work

Capturing the costs is our starting point, but we also need to organize these costs by the WBS to compare them against the budgeted cost for each of these WBS elements. In Figure 4.4, we can summarize these costs at the intersection of the WBS and the OBS. This is the place in the Responsibility Assignment Matrix where a person is assigned accountability for producing the deliverables for that WBS element at the planned cost.[12] This is the *single point of integrative responsibility* for that work and the place where the focus is on managing the project.[13] The assessment of the performance of this work includes the hours consumed by the labor and the cost of the materials needed to produce the outcomes. This information is used in the next step to determine any variances in cost and schedule, and will answer such questions as "What did you do with my money?" and "Did you produce what you planned to produce for the budget you planned to spend?" These are serious questions for any project manager, more so when we are spending other people's money.

A Checklist for Project Accounting

If we are spending other people's money, we need to account for the money and how we are spending it. If it is our own money, we probably should do the same thing. Here are some questions to ask to determine how to be good stewards of the money we have been given for the project:

> ➤ Do we have access to cost data from a reliable source? The time card system or the accounting system is the logical choice. If we don't have a time-keeping system, how can we determine the work effort applied to the work packages? This information is important to determine our future capacity for work.

> ➤ Do we account for cost in the same way we budget for cost? This means we can separate labor from material. If we have material, when do we pay our invoices and record that payment against our budget?

> ➤ Can we assign costs—both budgeted and actual—to a specific work package defined in the schedule with a WBS number and a specific organizational element? Both are needed to assess how we are spending the money.

> ➤ Do all our individual budgets at the WP level add up to the project budget? We are back to the all-in concept.

> ➤ Do we keep records to show accountability for all the material purchased for the project, including any leftover inventory?

Execute Project
Performance Analysis

Now that we have a budget for the planned project, we can collect the actual costs for performing the work using that budget, guided by the schedule for the work in the planned sequence. We can measure progress to our plan using physical percent complete and the cost to reach that physical percent complete. We will use this information to make management decisions, which is what project management is all about. Because *manage* is a verb, we need to take actions to keep the project going as planned or change how the project is planned.

Determine Variances for the Work Processes

We need to ensure that both significant schedule and cost variances are analyzed, at least monthly, at a level of detail required to manage the effort. This "at least monthly" answers the question, "How long are you willing to wait before you find out you are late?" If you don't know you are late in enough time to take corrective actions, you are late. This periodic analysis must be done to enable management decision making and to take corrective actions in timely manner. Comparing the budget value of work completed to the budget value of work planned during a given period of time provides a valuable indication of schedule status in terms of dollars of work accomplished. If we are looking for a motivation for this approach, simply answer the question, "How long are we willing to wait before we find out we are late?" The assessment of the project's performance needs to be at intervals short enough to take corrective action before we are actually late.

The analysis of the project's performance usually begins at the cost level. This is an easy approach, and it is tangible evidence of performance. Looking at each work package in Figure 4.4, we can determine the cost performance of this work against the planned cost. If we are "on budget," there is hope that we might be "on schedule." If we are "off budget," it is an indication there is something unfavorable about our performance and we need to look further. This budget assessment comes directly from the accounting system—the time cards, invoices, expenses, labor reports, material costs, all the things that come from the accounting system for the actual costs that are compared to the budgeted cost for the planned work. Reconciling the budget with the actual costs gives us the cost variance we need to assess the cost performance of the project.

Cost variance (CV) starts with a comparison of the planned cost with the actual cost for a period of performance. We should not use the total cost or the cumulative CV as our first measure of performance. We should start with the variances for the current period. This variance is an indication of how well we are managing costs in the short term. The cumulative variance masks the variability we need to make management decisions. We have all experienced the result of ignoring the short-term results, assuming we will make it up in the long run. For example, we have decided to lose two pounds a week for the next fifteen weeks for a target loss of thirty pounds. In the first four weeks, we are close to our goal, two pounds every week. But in week five, we only lose one pound. Our first thought is that we will lose three pounds in week six to get back on track. Probably won't happen. Staying on budget requires continuous vigilance. Focus on the short term and the long term will be easier to adhere to. In the late 1970s, a mentor told me, "The project is lost a day at a time. Get off by a week, and you'll never make it up." It changed my view of the world.

The next step is the analysis of our schedule variance. The first thing we must face up to is that spending money as planned is not the same as staying on schedule as planned. The measure of schedule performance—and this can't be said enough—must use tangible evidence of physical progress to plan. One approach is to create milestones, stating what is to be delivered at a particular point in time.[14] This schedule variance (SV) may not clearly indicate whether scheduled milestones are being met because some work may have been performed out of sequence or ahead of schedule while other work has been delayed. This out-of-sequence work will not match up with the planned budget for that work. As well, the products from the out-of-sequence work may "age" as other parts of the project change requirements that would have been used to build the outcomes. Now rework is needed to correct this. Schedule variance does not indicate whether a completed activity is a critical event or if delays in completing an activity will affect the completion date of the project. If we think of milestones as deadlines, we are go-ing to be disappointed in our ability to manage the project. We need to remember Douglas Adams's statement from *The Salmon of Doubt,* "I love deadlines. I love the whooshing noise they make as they go by."[15] So we need measures of physical percent complete on the planned day and should not use these fixed rocks on the side of the road as signs of progress. They can be passed much too easily.

Here's an example of how to measure physical percent complete:

> ➤ We have a kitchen-remodeling project and our initial efforts are in the drafting shop, making drawings for this remodel based on the customer's requirements. Figure 4.3 is a "notional" WBS for this project.

> ➤ We have four weeks to produce twenty drawings for the kitchen renovation.

> ➤ Each drawing has the same level of difficulty and should take the same effort and duration to produce. Our cost is directly related to effort: hours worked equal labor costs.

> ➤ We plan to produce these drawings at an equal pace, over the four weeks, twenty drawings total, five drawings per week.

> ➤ We have a budget of $1,000 for all twenty drawings, with a budget per drawing of $50 a drawing.

> ➤ We assume that one person is doing this work, and this person is available 100 percent over the four-week period of performance.

There are three measures for the performance of the drawings for our kitchen remodeling project:

1. We have a planned value for this project effort. This is the budgeted cost for the planned outcomes for the work efforts at the time of as-sessment. The spending profile is linear, $250 per week for the four weeks, to produce five drawings each week, costing $50 each.

2. We have the actual cost of the work performed at the time of as-sessment. We can measure that cost by looking at the number of hours spent by the one person doing the work.

3. We know the physical percent complete for the work efforts by looking at the number of drawings produced at the end of some measurement period and comparing it against the planned number of drawings for that same period.

Notice the phrase, "at the time of assessment." This is critical. If we plan to spend $1,000 as the total budget for the work over a four-week period, this is the *planned value*. This is the budget to produce our twenty drawings with a cost of $50 per drawing. When we assess the performance of our efforts, we do that at a specific point in time. This point in time has a cumulative budget, and, we need to assess our cumulative performance and our cumulative actual costs all at the same time. Let's measure our progress at the halfway point, week two.

Our plan says we should have spent 50 percent of our budgeted cost: $500. This is naïve, of course, but it makes our calculations simple. This means that after two weeks of work, we planned to have spent $500 for ten drawings at $50 each. We can also assume—again naïvely—that over the course of the four weeks, the actual value of the product—the drawings—we are producing is growing linearly. So at the two-week point, our product should be worth 50 percent of the planned cost, or $500. We earned our budget in this simple-minded example. So now it's Friday of the second week of our four-week project. We planned to spend $500 and to "earn" $500 of value from the ten drawings at $50 each.

But on Friday of the second week, we delivered only eight of the planned ten drawings. We are clearly behind schedule. We also discover that for that first two weeks, we spent $50 each for the first seven drawings and $70 for the eighth drawing, and failed to produce drawings nine and ten. So we underspent our budget to produce less than our planned outcome. For these eight drawings, we spent $420 (seven times $50 plus one drawing at $70). Our planned cost was $500, so we are $80 under budget.

Let us do some calculations:

> ➤ Our cost variance (CV) for the two weeks is $500 – $420, or $80 favorable. We underspent by $80 for the current period of performance.

> ➤ But we really want to know what we got for the money we spent. So just measuring the budget compared to the actual doesn't tell us much. We need to measure how much we spent compared to how much "value" we produced.

> ➤ At the start of the project, we planned to spend $50 for each drawing. We assume that when we spend $50 for each drawing, they are "worth" $50 of value. This is not the business value; that's a different topic. The $50 is the *sunk cost* value. We planned to pay $50 each, let's just call their value $50.

> ➤ For our total of ten drawings, we should have "earned" $500: ten drawings at $50 budget and $50 value.

> ➤ At the end of the two weeks, this is not the case. We produced only eight drawings, so we "earned" only $400 worth of value compared to our planned $500. We also spent $420 to produce those eight drawings. If we had produced the eight drawings at our planned cost, it would have cost us $400—eight drawings at $50 each, but we actually spent $420 to get our eight drawings.

> ➤ Not only did we not produce the planned number of drawings, but the ones we did produce cost more than we planned.

This type of analysis is much different from the simple cost and schedule assessment found on many projects. It is focused on measuring the production of value. This value is "earned" by measuring physical percent complete against the budget for that planned completion at the point in time when the assessment of progress is planned.

Take Corrective Action

These data and the calculations are interesting, but as project managers what we really need is the ability to forecast the future performance of our project given our past performance. To do this, we need to use additional measures. The first forecast calculation we need to perform is the Estimate at Completion (EAC), which is an estimate of how much the project is going to cost and how long it will take to reach done if we don't change anything we are currently doing. To arrive at our EAC, we first need to calculate the Cost Performance Index (CPI) using the following equation:

CPI = Value we "earned" / Actual cost to earn that value

= $400 / $420 = 0.95

This says we are earning only 95 percent of our investment in the work effort. For every dollar we spend, we get only 95 cents in "value" back. This is not a great way to run a project.

Once we have the CPI, we can calculate the EAC:

EAC = [Actual cost + (Budget at completion – Earned value)] / CPI

= [$420 + ($1,000 – $400)] / 0.95

= $1,073

This tells us that if we keep going at our current rate, we will overrun our original budget by $73.

But that's not the real problem. Let's see how late we are going to be. Let's calculate our Schedule Performance Index (SPI):

SPI = Earned value / Planned budget for the project

= $420 / $500

= 0.84

This says our schedule efficiency is only 84 percent of what it needs to be to complete on our planned four-week schedule. Let us look at the impact of this forecast on our planned completion date. We had planned four weeks for the total project, twenty working days, so the forecast completion duration can be calculated using the SPI:

Estimated completion duration = Planned duration / SPI

= 20 days / 0.84

= 23 days

We are forecasting we will be three days late and $73 over budget if we don't make changes to how the drawing project is executed.

Here's a quick summary of the management report we owe to the customer:

> ➤ At the end of two weeks—halfway through—we are missing two of the ten planned drawings.

> ➤ We spent more than our planned budget for the eight drawings we did deliver. For those eight drawings, we should have spent $400. But we spent $420 because the last drawing cost $70 instead of the planned $50.

> ➤ We produced fewer drawings than we planned. We were supposed to produce ten drawings in the first two weeks. But we produced only eight drawings during that period.

> ➤ We produced less than planned and spent more for what we produced than we planned.

> ➤ We are now late—eight drawings instead of ten—and we are over budget $420 instead of our planned $400 for those eight drawings.

If we don't do anything, we will be over budget by $73 and late by three days. What are our options? As project manager, these are our logical choices:

> ➤ We can catch up by producing more drawings at a lower cost. This means producing the remaining twelve drawings for the remaining $580; or $48 for each of the remaining drawings instead of the planned $50 each.

> ➤ We can keep on the current schedule, overrun by three days, and spend more money.

> ➤ There is no way to both get back on budget and back on schedule unless we produce the remaining drawings for less than we had planned and at the same time produce more drawings than we planned in the remaining weeks.

> ➤ We need to become more efficient at producing the drawings at a lower cost to stay on schedule and stay on budget.

This is also the conversation that, as project managers, we need to have periodically with the project team. By periodically, I mean weekly on any project of small to moderate size like this one; monthly is an absolute minimum for a project of any size. Measuring efficiency is the best indicator of project performance and should be done before measuring cost and schedule performance. Using this measure of efficiency, we can calculate schedule delays and budget overages from the assessment of physical percent complete.

Conduct a Performance Analysis Checklist

Once we have our baselined project schedule and budget and measurements of the cost and schedule performance of this baseline, we can look at the variances and take corrective actions to keep the project going as planned. Here are the questions you need to ask to do just that:

1. Do we analyze our performance in a consistent and systematic manner? Or do we use ad hoc processes to determine if we are on budget, on schedule, and meeting specifications?

2. Do we use objective results from our work to assess the performance of that work? Is there tangible evidence from each work package that the result met the requirements for the singular outcome?

3. Can we evaluate the impact of variances on cost and schedule in a way that provides actionable information to the decision makers? Without actionable information, it might be nice to know something, but we won't know what to do about it.

4. Do we have visibility to the root cause of the variance so we can take action to prevent it in the future? Once the root cause has been determined, do we have the ability to track the changes needed through resolution to be certain the cause of the variance has been eliminated?

5. With the current performance data, can we forecast our Estimate to Complete for the schedule and our Estimate at Completion for the total project cost? Are these estimates based on our

performance to date, actual cost to date, knowledgeable projections of our future performance, and any estimates of cost for the remaining work?

Record Revisions and Maintain Data

Continuing with our simple kitchen remodeling drawing production project, let us look at the data we have gathered and how we can manage changes to our work activities now that we know we are late and possibly over budget:

> ➤ Planned cost from our WBS for each deliverable includes labor and materials. The schedule for the production of the outcomes needs to be adjusted to either stay on budget or stay on schedule, but probably not both.

> ➤ Any changes to the schedule must assess the impact on the promised dates and the cost to produce those deliverables.

> ➤ Measures of Performance are assigned to each of the deliverables to confirm they are compliant with the technical requirements. Variances that result from this assessment require corrective actions to put the project back on schedule and on budget.

> ➤ The corrective actions we need to take must be recorded so that all participants understand what we are going to do next. Approval for these changes may involve the customer; it will certainly involve the project manager and those accountable for producing the outcomes. All must agree that any changes that result from the corrective actions will produce the desired outcome.

> ➤ Performance forecasts from the calculations for our new cost and schedule estimates must be published, reviewed, and approved by the project participants. There can be no surprises, or "I told you so," or worse yet, "I told you but you didn't understand."

This is the raw material needed for making management decisions. To make credible decisions, the data must have integrity. The data must be trustworthy. To be trustworthy, we need to know the provenance of the data. Where did the data come from, how was the information collected, how was it changed, who changed it, and why was it changed? Can we trace these changes through the life of the data?

Once we make a management decision to do something about our unfavorable performance to date, a change of some kind is needed. This can be a change in the schedule, a change in the budget, a change in the scope of the project, or even a change in the technical performance of the outcomes from our work effort. Whatever the change is, we must document it using a Change Control Management process, which entails asking ourselves the following questions:

1. Are authorized changes incorporated in a timely manner?

2. Are all the budgets, schedules, and other elements updated to reflect the approved change?

3. Are all the changes in budget and schedule reconciled with the customer's expectations?

4. If the approved changes result in schedule or budget overruns, has the customer acknowledged this outcome?

Looking Back

The five processes needed for the governance of the project provide the framework for applying the principles and practices. These process areas have specific outcomes that must be in place for success:

> ➤ Organizing the project requires that we define the deliverables with a work breakdown structure (WBS) and an organizational breakdown structure (OBS) for the resources performing the work.

> ➤ Planning and budgeting for the work requires that we assign the budget at the intersection of the OBS and WBS, as shown in Figure 4.4. With this budget and the defined work from the WBS dictionary, we can schedule the work in the proper sequence to produce our desired outcomes. This schedule and the assigned

budget identify the physical products. We need meaningful indicators of progress using milestones and technical performance goals to measure physical percent complete. The result of this effort is the Performance Measurement Baseline (PMB).

> ➤ With the PMB, we can capture the cost of performing the work. With this information, our next step is to assess these costs and the measures of physical percent complete to determine our progress to plan. This analysis of cost, schedule, and technical performance must be performed frequently to allow time to take corrective actions.

> ➤ With our measures of physical percent complete, we can forecast the final cost and completion dates using simple algebra. This provides information not available with traditional cost and schedule assessments.

What's Ahead?

With our principles, practices, and processes in place, we can now go to work. In the coming chapters, we will apply them to three projects that are simplified versions of actual projects. We will start with the needed capabilities; develop the requirement, then the plan and the schedule, and the measures of performance; identify risks and their handling; and establish the Performance Measurement Baseline. With everything in place, we will execute the project, generate some variances, and take corrective actions to put the project back on track.

These three projects will cover a broad range of domains:

> ➤ Remodel a home kitchen.

> ➤ Deploy an enterprise IT system that needs integration with legacy systems.

> ➤ Develop a new product that integrates hardware and software.

CHAPTER 5

Project Management Execution

Successful projects produce measurable value to the customer by delivering capabilities needed to fulfill a mission or strategy of the business or organization. These capabilities are assessed through their Measures of Effectiveness. During the execution of the project, process provides guidance for the principles and practices needed for success. In this chapter, we will execute three simplified, hypothetical, but real-world projects to see how to apply the principles, practices, and processes across each project: (1) a simple project using commercial off-the-shelf products, integrated into a system; (2) a tailored project from components, installed in a customer framework; and (3) an enterprise system integration project:

1. **A Personal Unmanned Aerial Vehicle (UAV).** Using commercial off-the-shelf parts, the Internet community, and some mechanical, electrical, and software skills, a UAV capable of flying around a park, following a person on a bike, and taking video can be assembled for under $1,000.

2. **A Kitchen Remodel.** For a fifteen-year-old house that currently has a "builder grade" kitchen: Using a kitchen designer and a general contractor, we want to replace the old kitchen with new "everything," while minimizing the structural impact on the home. A typical kitchen remodel, with top-shelf built-in appliances, and name-brand gas range and oven, really nice countertops (granite), hardwood floors, a wine bar, a coffee bar, and really cool light runs around $60,000. So this is a nontrivial investment for most homeowners. Managing this project is important to your pocketbook as well as to marital relations.

3. **A Health Insurance Provider ERP System.** A collection of legacy IT applications will be consolidated in the commercial off-the-shelf product by migrating existing providers and clients to the new system, while maintaining the operation of the legacy system. An "off-the-shelf" claims processing system, with integration of legacy systems, a moderate amount of customization, migration of all the legacy records, training, rollout, and go live will run about $100 million for a large insurance firm with several billion in revenue. This is a serious project, one that "bets the company" on its success. Proper management is a critical success factor for all involved.

Each project will apply the Five Immutable Practices, guided by the Five Immutable Principles, using the Five Processes. We will use them to develop the results for each of these projects. Each principle, practice, and process is presented for each project so you can see how each is applied to the project and how the three elements work together to create a successful result. Each project will offer a complete solution, with an end-to-end outcome. For comparison, figures at the end of the chapter will connect the dots between each of the principles, practices, and processes across each project. But for now, let's focus on one project at a time.

Before we start, let's look at Figure 5.1, which connects the principles, practices, and processes and see how they can be tailored to fit the domain, paradigm, and needs of the three sample projects.

In Chapters 2, 3, and 4, the principles, practices, and processes were presented as lists of elements with their outcomes. In this chapter, we will describe the three projects using a "storytelling" approach. This is a powerful concept used in many domains, under different names. On large government programs, the Concept of Operations (ConOps) tells the story of the characteristics of a proposed system from the point of view of an individual who will use that system. Its purpose is to communicate the quantitative and qualitative characteristics of the system to all stakeholders. These capabilities describe what the stakeholders can do with the outcomes of the project to improve their business or fulfill a mission.

FIGURE 5.1 Relationships among the Five Principles, Practices, and Processes.

	Principles	Practices	Processes
1	What does "done" look like?	Identify capabilities needed for project success.	Organize all the participants in the project.
2	How do we get to "done"?	Identify requirements that fulfill the needed capabilities.	Plan, budget, and schedule all the work on the project.
3	Do we have enough resources?	Develop Performance Baseline showing the sequence of work, and the resources and deliverables that implement the requirements.	Account for all project costs.
4	What are the impediments to progress?	Execute Performance Measurement Baseline for the work packages in the planned sequence.	Analyze cost and schedule variances and take corrective actions.
5	How do we measure progress?	Apply Continuous Risk Management to all activities in the project.	Revise and maintain any changes to cost, schedule, requirements, and capabilities.

In software projects, use cases and scenarios tell the story of the series of steps to be performed by the system and the participants to accomplish some outcome. Without this description of the capabilities, the customer has no way of knowing if the technical and operational aspects of the project will be of any value. In the end, without a clear and concise narrative or graphical description of what capabilities will be delivered and how these capabilities provide value, no one on the project knows what "done" looks like.

In our kitchen remodel project, use case and scenarios would not be particularly useful. Neither would a Concept of Operation. In this case, the interactions between the "equipment" and the user provide the best description of what capabilities are needed. The "user" is the cook, the outcome is food and beverages, and the guests of the dinner party are the consumers of those products. This is an experience-based statement of the needed capabilities, rather than a technical or operational description. The UAV and ERP project have more of a technical and operational approach, since they are both heavily dependent on technical performance for their success.

So let's get started by telling the story of our first project, the personal UAV.

Personal Unmanned Aerial Vehicle

A recent newspaper article told a story about a film company using an unmanned aerial vehicle (UAV) to photograph our downtown pedestrian mall for advertising. This story also described farmers using UAVs for cattle tracking, crop surveillance, and spot spraying. UAVs are used for inspections of chimneys and roofs, cooling towers, power lines, and wind turbine blades, as well as for construction progress photography, preconstruction surveys, wildlife filming, and sports coverage. These machines can be purchased or assembled from parts. This sample project calls for assembling a UAV from parts. It will be used for making videos of our cycle club members riding their mountain bikes on local trails. The FAA does not allow personal UAVs to fly higher than 400 feet above ground level (AGL), and they must stay in sight of the operator, so we'll establish that as a "hard" requirement. Our UAV will be autonomous while following us, so technically we are the "operator" with an *abort and land immediately* switch.

"Done," Capabilities, and Organization

We want a small helicopter UAV that can take high-definition (HD) video of us riding our mountain bikes, follow us on the trails after being launched, and fly for an hour and land safely. Once on the ground, we want to upload the video to our laptop so we can see and post our beautiful ride and amazing single-track cycling skills on the web for all to see. We could buy a $250 device that can do some simple things, but it will be more fun to build one from scratch using our hardware, software, mechanical engineering, and project management skills.

Because this is going to be a personal project, organizing it is simple. A small group—maybe two or three—of qualified people will be on the team. We will pool our money with a target budget of $750 for a fully functioning UAV with all the features we could ever want. Our skills need to be focused on the assembly and configuration rather than design and development, since all the parts can be purchased from standard sources.

The project will be "done" in stages:

1. Identify suitable components that can be assembled into a functional UAV. This includes the airframe, propulsion system, power system, flight software, ground control software, camera, GPS (Global Positioning System) needed for guidance, and the remote control hardware and software for flying the UAV.

2. Assemble these parts into a workable UAV and confirm they all work together reliably and provide all the capabilities as advertised by their suppliers.

3. Learn to fly under manual control in the park, without crashing too often. These flights will use the stability control, so once the UAV has been assembled, trimmed to fly straight and level and can follow the commands from ground control, the "pilot"

should be able to control the UAV with ease. The stability control software and hardware allows the pilot to concentrate on moving the UAV around the park without worrying about wind gusts upsetting the aircraft.

4. Add the camera and the GPS navigation module and we're ready to try autonomous flights in the park. Program the autonomous software to fly around the perimeter of the park and come back and land in front of us. This mode works using the GPS to sense where the UAV is in both altitude and position over the ground, just like the GPS mapping capability in a car or your smart phone.

5. Learn to define the track for the desired route in order to add "locator beacon" hardware and software so the UAV can follow a moving object on the ground.

6. Have the UAV follow us around the perimeter of the park for more testing and integration.

7. Add some simple command signals to "land," "hold position," "come home," and try out the UAV outside the park.

These capabilities need to fit inside a $1,000 budget. Our "team" needs to agree who rides the bike with the locator beacon, who controls the launch and monitoring of the UAV, who takes notes on what went wrong, and as a team how we are going to take steps to improve the outcomes. We are all engineers either by profession or experience, so working in a team comes naturally.

Since there are working examples of commercial UAVs for farmers, power companies, and other uses, we know it can be done. We just have to stick with the project long enough to make ours work as well. This means we need to seek the guidance of others so we don't have to discover all the problems by ourselves. Radio controller airplane clubs are the place to start. People with experience in the UAV hardware and software are another. And they can be found on the web in forums for UAVs.

Getting to "Done"—Requirements, Planning, Scheduling, and Budgeting

For our mountain biking needs, an autonomous video-equipped UAV is a well-defined project with clear and concise capabilities, requirements, and an easily developed schedule and budget. Why? Because there are numerous examples of these types of machines commercially available. They range in price from $1,000 to tens of thousands of dollars. All we have to do is look at the capabilities, configurations, and lists of features and decide what we want in our UAV.

Nevertheless, there are several incremental approaches here. The first is to film "downhill" riding. This is a short course, where the rider follows a path down a steep mountainside, with jumps, turns, and more jumps. The dimensions of the course are fixed and can be entered into the UAV's GPS navigation software. The UAV would "hover" over a spot, detect a rider coming, and follow that rider down the hill. The trail-following UAV needs more sensors to know the trail, follow the rider, and avoid obstacles, like trees, that might be in the way.

So let's start our list of technical requirements and develop a plan to deliver them:

> First is the ability to launch the UAV and have it follow us autonomously. Out on the trail, there is no room for a "pilot" to start the flight launch process. We ride narrow tracks (single track) in the mountains, so the UAV has to be able to know where we are, follow us as we ride, and land safely when we reach our destination. This capability will have to be developed incrementally, so the technical features can be added incrementally as well.
>
> The first technical requirement is to develop a platform that can be flown under remote control, like any other remotely controlled model airplane. Stability control is the key to this. Flying a helicopter UAV without built-in stability control results in a very short-lived vehicle, because it will crash often. Once stability control is installed, the UAV moves from being a backyard toy to a platform for doing real work.

> ➤ The UAV has to have an HD video camera with enough storage to hold enough imagery to make the result interesting—at least fifteen minutes of riding.

> ➤ Because the UAV is battery powered, it must be capable of flying, videoing, navigating, and landing for a reasonable amount of time on a single battery charge—twenty to thirty minutes.

> ➤ Navigation and tracking also need to be sensor driven. A locator beacon is one option. Another is map following. Most mountain bike trails are available from popular mapping sites, complete with elevation charts and details of the trail.

Resources, Performance Measurement, and Cost Accounting

Our UAV project's resources consist of suppliers and the tools needed to assemble and test the result. This is a small project that integrates high-technology components, guided by the assembly instructions. The primary resource is the "customer support" technicians for the purchased components. This is a selection criterion for some components. The Internet is the first place to look, not just for the components but also for the ratings of the customer support of each supplier. This concept can be extended to almost any "off-the-shelf" procurement. In the end, customer service is likely to be the most important "product" that is purchased in mature product domains.

The budget for our UAV is straightforward and connected directly to the capabilities. The more we pay for something, the more likely it is that "something" will have better performance. So our cost accounting starts with an upper limit on the budget, and an allocation of that budget to the needed capabilities.

We need:

> ➤ An airframe that holds the propulsion system and the power source. Can't fly without propulsion and power.

> ➤ The first-tier flight controls. These include the remote-control system, which gives directional and lift commands to the UAV.

With the airframe, propulsion, power, and remote control, we can start to learn how to fly before spending any more money.

> We quickly learn that flying the UAV in the park under manual control is much harder than it looks, so our next purchase is a flight stability system. This includes some sensors, some more software for our "central computer," and a few calibration and checkout processes. With our stabilization system installed, the UAV is much more controllable. It is a "fly-by-wire" machine now. We are flying the computer and the computer is flying the UAV, just like all other modern aircraft.

> Next is a navigation module that uses GPS to find the path to fly. This module can be uploaded with a flight plan, follow that flight plan, and return to the landing zone. Now we are getting closer to the autonomous vehicle that can follow us around the park.

> With that module integrated and tested, we now need a video feed so we can send back live pictures from the UAV flying around the park.

Impediments, Execution, and Performance Analysis

This project is about the assembly of commercial off-the-shelf components. The primary impediment to progress is the advanced understanding needed to select and integrate the components for the UAV. These impediments can be addressed straightforwardly—by reading the directions. This assumes we are qualified in this area, but that is behind us. We are hardware and software engineers with experience in integrating off-the-shelf components. This, of course, does not eliminate the impediments, but it does provide us with skills to deal with them. This is a critical understanding: If we are to manage a project, we should know something about the technology and how it is put to work to deliver a capability.

With our schedule for delivering the capabilities, we can identify the sequence of purchases, assembly, testing, and first operations.

Measuring Progress, Managing Risk, and Revising Our Plan

Progress measurement is straightforward. We buy parts from the web, assemble them following the instructions, run all the tests, and try out the assembled system in the park. Progress is measured by working capabilities—simple flying, stability control flying, flying a route, flying with a video feed along the route, following the rider with the "locator" while videoing the ride.

The primary risks involve the improper assembly of the parts, failure to read the instructions, and our low skill in actually flying the UAV. These risks can all be addressed through "learning." These are reducible risks, with information we can find from a variety of sources. This information reduces uncertainty and the resulting risk. This information is usually free, which is not true for our next two projects.

Wrap-Up of the Personal UAV Project

The story of our UAV was simple: We want to build and fly a machine that can follow us on the trail, take videos so we can see what happened, do this for thirty minutes or so, all using off-the-shelf hardware and software. The skills of our team include software development, mechanical engineering, electrical engineering, and the ability to read instructions and debug the machine after we don't follow the instructions.

The plan is simple; follow the instructions. Timing is simple; we have evenings and weekends to work on our project, no real deadline. This is a "hobby" project, but it does require organizing, planning, funding, and actual "touch labor" to get the UAV to work. There are no real impediments beyond our own capabilities. Since our team members all have "day jobs" performing the needed skills, there is little doubt we can get the UAV to work. Not learning to fly the UAV before we break it is the primary risk, but once the stabilization and autopilot hardware and software are installed, that risk goes down.

Kitchen Remodel

Our current kitchen is going on fifteen years old. It was a "builder's quality" kitchen with builder appliances, a standard layout, and tract-home feel. We wanted an upgrade that made use of modern appliances, had a better layout within the framing structure of the home, and provided capabilities not found in the current design. At the start of the project, appliances were available that had much higher efficiency ratings. The prices for restaurant-quality cooking appliances were coming down, and the style of modern kitchens was moving from "cooking-centric" to "entertaining-centric" layouts, where the kitchen is the focus of the party, not the dining area.

What Does "Done" Look Like?

The answer is simple:

> ➤ The old kitchen is gone and the new kitchen with new "everything" is installed without collateral damage to any other part of the house.

> ➤ This is all done close to our planned budget and planned time frame.

What this really means is that once we decide on what the kitchen will look like, there will be no surprises, it will all be done according to plan, and the "stakeholder" will be happy.

"Done," Capabilities, and Organizing the Kitchen Project

When spending your own money, one good question to ask is, "Why are we doing things?" Once we decided to move forward with the remodel project, these capabilities were the focus of our efforts:

> ➤ Space, access, and flow to host dinner parties for twelve couples, members of our supper club.

> Appliances that exceed the energy savings guidelines of modern kitchens.

> The ability to cook three main courses at the same time in the same room for large dinner parties.

> Increased storage for cooking utensils and serving dishes.

With these capabilities, the next step is to organize to get the kitchen done. This begins with:

> Engaging a kitchen designer to help us select cabinet styles, colors, and layout.

> Engaging a general contractor (GC) to provide all the work except the installation of cabinets and appliances. There will be demolition work as well as installation, so coordinating all the subcontractors, including the kitchen designer, is needed to ensure that everyone knows the proper roles and responsibilities, has availability to work on this project, has the same quality standards, has all the licenses and permits needed to work on site, and agrees on the business arrangements. The GC is the single point of contact for this project. Financially, the GC might not be the only direct pay resource, but the GC is in charge of how the work is planned and executed.

The kitchen remodel organization is straightforward:

> A general contractor is going to do the heavy lifting for the construction.

> A few subcontractors are involved, including a cabinet designer, appliance supplier, and countertop supplier.

> The trades, such as electrical, plumbing, and flooring, are provided through the general contractor, are managed by the GC, and provide their services in a transparent manner.

> Last, there are the stakeholders. In this case, there is only one stakeholder—the "monarch" of our kitchen.

Getting to "Done"—Requirements, Planning, Scheduling, and Budgeting

The kitchen remodel is a straightforward project, ignoring for the moment any unforeseen complications. It is assumed that we will not rearrange any of the structural aspects of the kitchen in this project, which means we will leave the structural walls where they are, leave the plumbing for the most part where it is, move utility electrical around to be more convenient, and upgrade the appliance electrical to better fit the modern code. The requirements for the contents of the kitchen and the planning and scheduling start with the following:

> ➤ Picking out cabinets, appliances, countertops, backsplash, flooring, plumbing fixtures, and a bunch of detailed "gadgets."

> ➤ Deciding when we need the final kitchen and working backward six to eight weeks. The work starts with the demolition of the existing kitchen, so we need to also decide where to cook in the meantime.

> ➤ Starting with the cabinets, because they are the "signature" of the kitchen. This means engaging a cabinet designer once we've seen sample kitchens we liked and have narrowed down the style and general color and finish.

Resources, Performance Measurement, and Cost Accounting

Now we're getting to the hard part, at least for this project. There is a budget for the kitchen. There is some margin in the budget, but there is a "not to exceed" cost. Resources may be a problem, because special skills—cabinet installers—may be hard to come by. General tradesmen are usually available. Countertop tradesmen are usually more specialized, and we wanted some unique features, so the general contractor was assigned the task of using his best people for that. Appliance consultants are provided by the appliance vendors, so that's simple;

the same holds for lighting and plumbing fixtures. The resource plan is straightforward again:

> Cabinet shop has designers.

> Plumbing fixture shop has designers that can connect with the cabinets for color and style.

> Appliance store offers options for every appliance—range, oven, microwave, refrigerator, freezer, and the ever-critical wine cooler. It was decided up front to have a separate built-in refrigerator/freezer.

Performance measures of the kitchen crew start with the planned completion date and the incremental completion of the components of the kitchen. "Demo'ing" the existing kitchen must be done first. The schedule for that drives the rest of the job. The budget for all the work was worked out in advance, with margin for both cost and schedule. This is usually a "not to exceed" type budget. The costs of materials, appliances, and other tangible items are easy to determine. The surprises found during the work are not. For that, we'll need budget margin within our "not to exceed" number to cover these overages.

Impediments, Execution, and Performance Analysis

Impediments to progress are, for the most part, easily identified. No permits are needed because there are no structural changes. Lead times for appliances are reasonable. Lighting and plumbing fixtures are in stock. Prices are established within tolerance ranges, so the budget looks credible. Labor estimates are credible, since each craft has done kitchens like this before.

What is unknown is what is behind the wallboard in the current kitchen. This is a semi-custom house, built at the height of the building boom, by crews that came and went without a lot of continuity. So when the wallboard is ripped off, we'll see what's underneath and how much impact that will have on cost and schedule. On the actual project, it turned out that the floor joists for the upper floor were going the wrong way, so the vent for the range hood had to be specially built, because it had to run through four joists to reach to the outside wall. The wall behind the range was not to code—too narrow—and the gas line and oven back intruded into the wall. Also, the existing pantry had a return duct intruding into the space that had to be modified so the cabinets that replaced the pantry and the separate built-in freezer would fit flush with the cabinet depth.

Could these impediments have been known before we started? Probably not. You have to rip off the wallboard to see these code violations. The same was true of some electrical code violations that required repair.

Measuring Progress, Managing Risk, and Revising Our Plan

So we have a plan, a budget, and a firm idea of what the final kitchen will look like. We are convinced it will provide the needed capabilities when done, so let's go to work. Use the planned sequence of work—empty the current kitchen, remove the appliances, demolish the cabinets, rip the wallboard off—but first close off the kitchen with plastic to protect the rest of the house from the huge mess the work will create.

With the cabinet plan, measure precisely the fit of the upper and lower cabinets along the wall. Measure twice, even three times, because once the cabinets are ordered we're committed. The same is true for the built-in appliances. These are counter depth, ordered from the dealer, but built in Germany. The sizes are standard, but the door fronts—so they look like cabinets—are custom-made by the cabinet shop. Electrical and plumbing layouts for the refrigerator and freezer have to be defined—once they are installed there is no "uninstalling" or moving them. They are "built-ins," and that means permanent built-ins! Wine refrigerator is easier, because it can slide out from under its countertop.

Countertops are another sensitive topic. There are hundreds of choices of stone: granite for the perimeter countertops, something more unusual for the island. Cost for granite is controlled by the volume of stone in the quarry: the more stone in the ground, the lower the price. It is a pure commodity pricing strategy. So find something that fits the design but is low cost, and spend the rest on a smaller piece, but more expensive. So find the right combination of "common" and "unique," engage the firm that will finish and install the countertops, and schedule the workers to come once the lower cabinets are installed.

Demolition is simple, just like on TV. Get a sledgehammer, swing away, don't hurt yourself. Try not to ding the hardwood floor even though it has to be refinished. Electrical boxes can be relocated now, new wiring pulled, drains and water feeds moved to the right places, and "ugly" pieces of the room cleaned up.

Wrap-Up of the Kitchen Project

The complexity of the kitchen project is more than the UAV, but still low compared to the next project. No structural changes, no major electrical or plumbing other than cleanup, semi-custom cabinets, picked out of a catalog, appliances picked out of a catalog as well, everything else "store-bought." Work processes are serial—rip stuff out, fix what needs to be fixed after stuff has been ripped out, install new stuff, hook it up, test it out, clean up the mess. The principles, practices, and processes for managing a kitchen rebuild type of project are straightforward:

> ➤ Develop an overall "look and feel" of the kitchen, the style of the cabinets, colors, and trim. Decide on the appliances and other fixtures. Confirm the layout and capacities of the equipment that can be the foundation of a moderate-sized dinner party, and the primary stakeholder will be happy in the long term with all the choices.

> ➤ Select the right contractors, who can work with each other, understand the goal of the kitchen, and are available for work.

> ➤ Prepare for any delays once the walls are exposed, and have solutions, including workarounds, to keep the project moving.

> ➤ Plan progress measures in "big chunks." Kitchen emptied, wallboard removed, electrical and plumbing corrected, wallboard back, cabinets installed, appliances installed, countertops installed, all finish work complete.

Health Insurance Provider
Network Application Migration

We're on the third of our three sample projects showing how to tailor the principles, practices, and processes of Performance-Based Project Management. This project is an Enterprise Resource Planning (ERP) project; in this case, an IT effort that starts with a collection of legacy applications that form the basis for enrolling healthcare providers in an insurance network. If we look back to Figure 2.2, we can see the "enrollment" process is needed early on as part of a larger conversion effort. The new system will ultimately replace the collection of legacy systems, but during the transition period, normal business operations will be conducted using these legacy systems. The project allows physicians and hospitals to "enroll" as healthcare providers using the insurance company's benefit plan. Patients cannot be "provided" healthcare without the "providers" knowing that they are covered.

The focus of the project is not on the technology, but on the operational processes needed to deliver the project. The technology will be provided by a commercial off-the-shelf (COTS) product. Data migration, workflow processes, management training, customer training, and data integrity validation are all part of the migration process.

"Done," Capabilities, and Organizing the ERP Project

Done for this project is easy to define. The legacy systems are replaced with a single integrated enterprise system capable of enrolled providers for 15 percent less than the legacy systems. It's really that simple, even for a large enterprise IT project. To begin, write a few simple, measurable, clear, and concise statements describing what this will look like:

> ➤ Replace legacy systems with an integrated system for provider enrollment.

> ➤ Reduce transaction costs by 15 percent for end-to-end activities—from provider identification to provider payment.

> Transfer data from all legacy systems to a single integrated database, while scrubbing providers' network content to ensure that no provider is misplaced and all data are verified against all past transactions and providers.

> Deploy web-based provider enrollment interface with the same baseline functionality, at the very least, as the heavier interface offered.

> Deploy portable device interfaces for iOS- and Android-based tablets with the same functionality as the legacy system.

The core activity of this project is to determine the cost to stay on schedule as well as to verify that the delivered capabilities provide the planned value to the enterprise. So let's start with confirming what "done" looks like and develop a plan, schedule, and budget to reach "done."

With the legacy systems in place, the organization of the project is based on employing existing staff, processes, and technology. Our goal is to transition the existing technology to a new technology using the current staff. This requires subject-matter experts currently in place to guide the transition. Leaders of each business process are accountable for the activities needed to successfully make this transition.

Getting to "Done"—Requirements, Planning, Scheduling, and Budgeting

The description of "done" requires seamless transition from the legacy systems to the new system, starting with the provider network enrollment processes. This capability allows the business to start saving money while maintaining the same customer-facing interface. The challenge is to develop a clear and concise plan, schedule, and budget for getting to the provider network capabilities. This means we don't need the full set of capabilities illustrated in Figure 2.2; rather, we can deploy these capabilities incrementally, allowing the business to take advantage of the capabilities as they emerge to deliver value from their investment. This does not mean the work is not done in sequence; it is. This is the planned delivery of incremental value to the customer that is the basis of all agile development processes. This notion of incremental delivery using Agile works in a variety of domains, not just software. Lean construction is one example popular today.[1]

To develop a plan, schedule, and budget, we need to know what business capabilities are needed and how they will be implemented using the technical and operational requirements. The requirements are for technology and processes based on the technology that fulfills the capabilities. We begin by stating the capabilities in the form of scenarios or use cases, just like our other two projects:

> Enroll providers in the new system using the same work processes as the legacy systems did.

> Migrate all legacy providers into the new system with 100 percent transparency, meaning no provider will know there is a new system.

> Once the new system is active, reduce the cost of enrolling a new provider by 15 percent compared to the legacy systems. This 15 percent reduction will come from lower customer support costs, transaction processing costs, error correction costs, and other operational costs associated with capturing, maintaining, and supporting the provider network.

Resources, Performance Measurement, and Cost Accounting

The acquisition and deployment of the technology can be handled by a systems integrator. The primary resources for this project are the subject-matter experts needed to ensure that the capabilities of the new system match those of the legacy system. This means the internal users of the system, those who operate the provider network management system, are the ones guiding the transition from legacy to new. These resources, of course, have "day jobs," which means their normal operational roles in the insurance company must still be accomplished. Therefore, resource planning must address the utilization of the operational staff and their reduced availability for normal work. This might mean backfilling staff, possibly outsourcing many of the day-to-day functions to staff augmentation firms, and so on. Without these subject-matter experts, the new system will represent what the vendor thinks the system should do—or worse, what the system is capable of doing in the absence of any external guidance.

With the staff in place to guide the deployment of the new system, the measures of performance are straightforward. "The system works like the legacy system." This means the processes, data, and outcomes of the new system are substantially the same as those of the legacy system. If the new system does not work like the legacy system, then that behavior must be benign. This approach to resource management is similar to operations management. The system being managed has to be operational in the end. So the resources must be capable of recognizing what *operational* means. These resources become the "owners" of the final system and, as such, become the "acceptors" of the capabilities of the final system.

Impediments, Execution, and Performance Analysis

The vendor doing the systems integration work now has the resources that can describe what "done" looks like. This removes many of the impediments to progress, as there is little room for interpretation of what to do or how to do it. The primary impediment is the availability of these resources.

With the subject-matter experts on the same team as the system integrators, measuring progress to plan means starting with the plan for deployment of the existing capabilities using the new system. This is done with the "make-a-list" methodology. We need a list of the current capabilities, evidence of what they do to the various elements involved in this activity, and the underlying processes used to produce each element. This starts with an as-is process flow for the legacy system and is a "build to" specification for the new system. The as-is process flow shows the people, processes, and tools used to perform the work of enrolling providers in the insurance network. An example of the as-is approach is shown in Figure 5.2.

FIGURE 5.2 As-is process flow in a provider network enrollment.

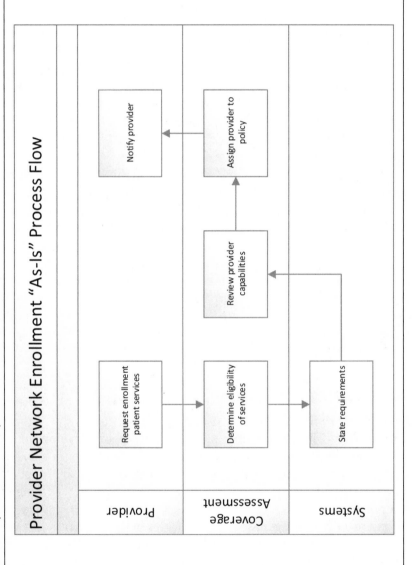

Provider Network Enrollment "As-Is" Process Flow

| Provider | Coverage Assessment | Systems |

Measuring Progress, Managing Risk, and Revising Our Plan

Using an as-is process flow such as the one illustrated in Figure 5.2, we can define how to measure progress. Each of the work activities must be in place for the provider network to have the capability of enrolling new providers. A schedule of when those capabilities will be available for verification can then be built by the system integrator. For each of the boxes in Figure 5.2 (and these are notional boxes), the subject-matter experts can show in detail what is now being done on the legacy system and verify that the new system is doing the same thing. This is a side-by-side comparison.

The risks associated with this approach lie in the ability of the current subject-matter experts to recognize that the new system is performing its job as the legacy system does and that they can convey any differences to the system integrator. This is a challenge because the subject-matter experts may or may not be able to communicate the technical details of what they only know as "operational" aspects of the system. This risk can be addressed through an interpreter, meaning someone who knows the new system, can learn the legacy system's operational aspects, and can work alongside the subject-matter experts to translate between the two systems.

Wrap-Up of the Health Insurance ERP Project

Modern enterprise IT projects usually start with a legacy system of some sort moving to an upgrade or replacement. Development of an IT solution "from scratch" is rare these days. Managing a transition project requires a careful approach to ensure that the result meets the business need, since the new system is usually based on a commercial off-the-shelf product. Customization of this product rarely returns value. Ensuring that the baseline capabilities of the COTS product meet the needs of the organization starts with the subject-matter experts defining the as-is processes and data. With this information, we can define the steps needed to replicate these processes and data in the new system as a baseline for the business operations.

Only then should new features be added. Making the transition to a new system, maintaining the continuity with existing users and adding new features creates unnecessary risk. A step-wise transition process ensures that the integrity of the legacy system is established before making it better. The new system can act as a platform for "making it better."

Looking Back

We took a deep dive in this chapter into the practices needed for success and applied them to three notional projects here. The following checklist can be applied to any project. We begin with the principles:

> Define what "done" looks like through storytelling.

> Show how we are going to get to "done" on time and on budget.

> Confirm that we have enough resources to reach "done."

> Identify any impediments that might be encountered along the way to "done," and specify how you are going to handle them.

> Determine how you are going to measure physical percent complete to ensure that progress is being made to plan.

Figure 5.3 illustrates how these principles were used on each of our three sample projects.

Next, we need to apply the Five Practices to the project:

> Identify the needed capabilities by listing what outcomes are required to implement your "story." What does the customer want the results of the project to do? These are the capabilities. The capabilities to process transactions at a lower cost is a capability. The ability to follow the rider on the trail is a capability. The ability to entertain thirty guests is a capability. These are the "reasons" for the project.

> Identify the baseline requirements using the technical and operational terms found on the project. These used to be called

FIGURE 5.3 Five Principles of project success for unmanned aerial vehicle, kitchen remòdel, and health insurance provider projects.

Five Principles of Project Success		
Unmanned Aerial Vehicle	Kitchen Remodel	Health Insurance Provider
1. What Does "Done" Look Like?		
■ Provide a low-cost, easy-to-operate UAV for surveillance of 1,000 acres of pasture land, occupied by cattle and horses.	■ Sufficient space, appliances, storage, and workflow to cook for dinner parties for 12 couples. ■ New kitchen increases the resale value of our home.	■ Replace the legacy system with a new system that can process enrollments at $0.07 versus the $0.12 in the current system.
2. How Can We Reach "Done"?		
■ Identify off-the-shelf components for hardware and software. ■ Assemble UAV in increments.	■ Pick out all components for kitchen. ■ Build schedule for 6- to 8-week work effort. ■ Start with important components, the cabinets.	■ Define current system data model. ■ Define interfaces and transition to test. ■ Define transition to business.
3. Do We Have Resources?		
■ Hardware test equipment on hand. ■ Software development platform installed. ■ Hardware and software skills available when needed.	■ General contractor will provide the needed resources. ■ Kitchen designer will provide needed resources.	■ Identify all skills needed for each work package. ■ Assign work packages' managers.
4. What Are the Impediments to Our Progress Toward "Done"?		
■ GPS not accurate enough for autonomous flight. ■ Weight exceeds lift capacity. ■ Battery life insufficient for ranch use.	■ Permits. ■ Hidden structural issues with the house. ■ Electrical capacity. ■ Price of appliances.	■ Missing subject-matter experts with capabilities to recognize the pitfalls along the way to reaching "done."
5. How Can We Measure Progress?		
■ Controlled flight. ■ Auto stability. ■ GPS integration. ■ Camera integration. ■ Initial autonomous flight test. ■ Autonomy within pasture boundaries.	■ Cabinets removed. ■ Appliances ordered. ■ Electrical system designed and ordered. ■ Cabinets installed. ■ Plumbing installed. ■ Appliances installed. ■ Flooring installed.	■ Capabilities defined on the master plan delivered in planned order. ■ Budget performance for each capability within limits. ■ Schedule performance for each capability within limits. ■ Capability verified against specification.

"feeds and speeds" in the mechanical world. Now with software intensive projects, except for the kitchen remodel, we need other words. Each technical and operational requirement must be traceable to a needed capability. Capabilities without requirements to fulfill them are widows. Requirements without a reason for being there are orphans. Technical and operational requirements are fulfilled by products and services. Transaction speed and cost, square footage for sitting and standing space, bandwidth and tracking signals are all technical or operational requirements.

> Develop the Performance Measurement Baseline by agreeing on the duration, roles, budget, outcomes, and how progress is going to be measured. "Plan the work and work the plan" is the overused phrase. But this is exactly what the PMB does for us. Without a plan we can't see where we are going and we can't recognize done when we get there.

> Execute the Performance Measurement Baseline by following the plan. Perform the work in the planned order, try to stay on budget, use the planned people for the planned work, and measure progress with tangible outcomes, not effort and cost.

> Perform Continuous Risk Management on all the work activities in the Performance Measurement Baseline.

Figure 5.4 illustrates how these practices were used on each of our three sample projects.

With the principles and practices in place, we need a governance process framework for managing the project:

> Organize the work and the resources performing the work by stating up front who is needed and when they are needed.

> Plan, schedule, and budget the work with simple or complex tools suited to the project. Write it down. Even sticky notes on the wall of the garage can be used for plans, schedules, and budgeting. Larger projects require larger tools—that's the only difference.

FIGURE 5.4 Five Practices of project success for unmanned aerial vehicle, kitchen remodel, and health insurance provider projects.

Five Practices of Project Success		
Unmanned Aerial Vehicle	Kitchen Remodel	Health Insurance Provider
1. Identify Needed Capabilities		
■ Fly around the park under autonomous control following the locator beacon. ■ Take video of us riding our mountain bikes around the park.	■ Space, access, and flow sufficient to host dinner parties for 12 couples. ■ Ability to cook 3 main courses at the same time in the same room. ■ Increased storage for cooking utensils and serving dishes.	■ Replace legacy systems with a commercial off-the-shelf integrated system. ■ Do this in a seamless manner, with no impact on external users—providers.
2. Identify Baseline Requirements		
■ Assemble the UAV from off-the-shelf components. ■ Test assembled system using "store-bought" equipment. ■ Keep costs under $1,000 for the complete system.	■ Cabinets ordered from catalog. ■ Built-in appliances bought from supplier. ■ Minimal structural changes to kitchen.	■ Enroll providers using same work processes. ■ Migrate all legacy providers with 100% transparency to external users. ■ Reduce cost of enrolling provider by 20%.
3. Develop the Performance Measurement Baseline		
■ Self-paced development possible in evening work efforts.	■ Work completed within 8 weeks.	■ Identify subject-matter experts for provider network transition and dedicate them to the project. ■ Define feature rollout plan using subject-matter experts for priorities.
4. Execute the Performance Measurement Baseline		
■ Instructions on assembly and test written for amateurs with some electronics and software skills.	■ Follow general contractor plan of directing subcontractors and purchase of appliances and cabinets.	■ Migrate legacy data. ■ Confirm all features in the new system operate identically to those in the legacy system.
5. Perform Continuous Risk Management		
■ Vehicle is "robust" enough to survive crashes while learning to fly. ■ "Return to home" mode allows safe landing and recovery.	■ Minimal impact on infrastructure may not be possible. ■ Identify workarounds before making any structural changes.	■ Verify parallel operations are identical before proceeding to the next step.

➤ Account for all the costs in performing the work by keeping track of the budget and the expenditures. It's that simple. Again, it is only a matter of scale. But this accounting process is not a measure of progress. It is only a measure of money planned and money spent.

➤ Analyze the performance of the work. That old phrase, "If you don't know where you're going, any path will take you there," is not true. If you don't know where you are going, you are lost. Measure progress with tangible evidence of the outcomes on the planned date for the planned budget.

➤ Make any needed revisions to the plans, budgets, or schedules for the work.

Figure 5.5 illustrates how these processes were used on each of our three sample projects.

Some General Observations

Project success, of course, starts with knowing what "done" looks like, how to get to "done," and the impediments along the way to "done." This last piece is critical. For each of our sample projects, the impediments can be discovered through the effort of others. There is no reason to do it alone or from scratch. Instead, find similar projects, and learn from them; try to understand the reasons for their success or failure.

The same is true for the requirements, plans, schedules, and budgets. Rarely is a project the first of its kind. Look around to see if there are similar projects. Search out the people who worked on those projects or any documentation from those projects in order to learn from them. This is one purpose of project management forums and the Project Management Institute (PMI) chapters. Sharing knowledge and experience is what project managers should do. This is a risk-reduction process. Learn from the mistakes and successes of others and pass that information on to others.

FIGURE 5.5 Five Processes of project success for unmanned aerial vehicle, kitchen remodel, and health insurance provider projects.

Five Processes of Project Success		
Unmanned Aerial Vehicle	Kitchen Remodel	Health Insurance Provider
1. Organizing		
▪ Assemble the sources for all the components of the UAV. ▪ Agree on who is doing what on the project—hardware, software, operations.	▪ Identify the general contractor and the subcontractors and have them agree on what "done" looks like.	▪ Assign existing subject-matter experts to guide the system integrator. ▪ Use current staff to verify new system works identically to the legacy system.
2. Planning, Budgeting, and Scheduling		
▪ Locate commercial off-the-shelf suppliers. ▪ Identify components that cost no more than $1,000.	▪ Qualify cabinet suppliers. ▪ Qualify general contractor. ▪ Establish total budget for materials and labor. ▪ Define sequence of work to minimize impact on household routines.	▪ Define sequence of capabilities for enrolling providers. ▪ Arrange conversion of data and work processes to ensure transparent impact on existing providers.
3. Project Accounting		
▪ Partition costs for maximum reuse of investments with upgrades and reuse.	▪ Allocate costs proportional to top-level components of the kitchen including appliances, cabinets, lighting, and installation.	▪ Define costs for each capability and confirm return on these costs for support of business case.
4. Project Performance Analysis		
▪ Measure component costs against "best price" available in the market.	▪ Measure installation costs versus planned installation time in hours and materials.	▪ Measure planned completion of conversion and hours needed against budget. ▪ Confirm that cost savings and process improvement benefits match planned cost.
5. Revisions and Data Management		
▪ Maintain cost and technical information for warranty.	▪ Maintain contractual information for general contractor and subcontractors for confirmation of invoices. ▪ Maintain warranty information for all purchases.	▪ Maintain baseline plan and budget for confirmation of business case fulfillment. ▪ Maintain data migration processes for confirmation of seamless transition.

What's Ahead?

With the principles, practices, and processes developed and applied to three sample projects, with a deep dive into the practices, we are now ready to look at the artifacts that are produced by Performance-Based Project Management. These artifacts start with the Statement of Work, which describes the items to be delivered. This can be a simple list of things the project will do, like those developed for the UAV project. Or this can be a more formal document in the form of specifications for operational and technical capabilities.

For any project to have a chance of success we need a plan and a schedule. The schedule shows us the path to reach "done," what work needs to be performed along the way, who is doing this work, and how much it is going to cost. Building this resource-loaded, budgeted schedule sounds like a lot of work, but without it we do not have visibility into the resource and funding risks associated with the project. Since we are spending other people's money, this is an important attribute for the success of our work. Once we have identified the risks, we need a Risk Management Plan, a Risk Register, and a connection to the schedule for handling these risks.

CHAPTER 6

Tailoring the Principles and Practices for Project Success

Now that the principles are in place and the processes to implement those practices have been defined, we can examine the details of these practices to determine how to successfully manage different types of projects. In the last chapter, we looked at three sample projects; now we need to go deeper to gain an understanding of why certain things were done and others were skipped over. We need to learn how we can adapt the practices to various kinds of projects.

For a quick review, let's look at the three elements of Performance-Based Project Management needed for project success:

1. **Principles.** We need to know what a project's final deliverables look like through the eyes of the customer or end user. We need to know what products or services we will be providing and how they will be used to fulfill a mission or business case. We need to understand how we will recognize these deliverables when they arrive and how we can we reduce any risks to the successful completion of the project.

2. **Practices.** Once we understand the capabilities the project will deliver, we need to know what technical and operational requirements are needed to enable these capabilities, how the project will be staffed, what the impediments to progress are, and how we will measure progress to our plan.

3. **Processes.** We need a set of governing processes to guide us in the work of managing the project. This includes organizing the project; planning, budgeting, and scheduling the work; accounting for the money and time required for that work; analyzing the variances that are part of the normal project processes; and maintaining and managing the changes to our plans, budgets, or deliverables.

These principles, practices, and processes are essential to the success of any project, no matter the domain. But the details of each of these can be applied in a graded manner to the project.

Tailoring the Practices to Fit the Project

It's time now to address the practical issue that one-size-does-not-fit-all project management situations. We need a way to tailor the elements of Performance-Based Project Management to fit the needs of the project and its participants. We cannot ignore or replace any of these elements because they are all needed for project success, but we need to recognize that the "fidelity" of the details may be different for different projects, domains, and contexts within each domain. We need a mechanism to distinguish between the levels of management rigor to be applied to various projects.

The principles should be obvious to anyone working on a project: We need to know what "done" looks like, how we are going to get there, what we need to reach our goal, what problems we are going to encounter, and how we are going to measure progress to our plan. The processes are straightforward as well, but the levels of detail can vary.

Let's focus first on tailoring the practices to the project. In the previous chapters, we developed the elements of the principles, practices, and processes, but let's summarize them here in preparation for the tailoring activities. We will then look at each practice and decide how to tailor it for three classes of projects:

1. Identify the needed system capabilities—what will we do with the results of the project in our business?

2. Establish the requirements baseline—what technical and operational requirements are needed to deliver the needed capabilities?

3. Establish the Performance Measurement Baseline—show the sequence of work and the cost of that work to produce the technical and operational products that fulfill the needed capabilities.

4. Execute this Performance Measurement Baseline—perform the work in the planned sequence to deliver the needed capabilities to the customer.

5. Performance Continuous Risk Management—during the execution of each of the four practices above, manage the risks that will inhibit their success.

Figures 6.1(a) and 6.1(b) contain the details of the first four practices. These figures can be used as a checklist to ensure that practices are being properly applied.

FIGURE 6.1(a) Activities needed to deliver capabilities and requirements baseline.

1. Identify Needed Systems Capabilities—Define the Measures of Effectiveness Performance-Based Project Management

Define Capabilities as Operational Concepts

Partition system capabilities into classes of service within operational scenarios or use cases.

Connect capabilities to system requirements in some traceable form to ensure that no capabilities are implemented by a requirement.

Define Measures of Effectiveness (MoE) for each capability in units meaningful to the decision makers.

Define through the master schedule the achievement of technical performance that fulfills each capability.

Define Operational Concepts with Scenarios or Use Cases

Define scenarios for each system capability to confirm the business case is being met or the mission requirements are being fulfilled.

Connect these scenarios to a map of how value is being delivered by the project.

Assess value flow through the map for each needed capability.

Identify capability mismatches and make corrections to improve overall value flow.

Assess Needs, Cost, and Risk of the Capability Simultaneously

Assign costs to each system element using a value process model.

Ensure that risk, probabilistic cost, and benefit performance attributes are defined.

Use cost, schedule, and technical performance probabilistic models to forecast potential risks to program performance.

Define Explicit, Balanced, and Feasible Alternatives

Make tradeoffs that connect cost, schedule, and technical performance in a single "trade space" model.

Measures of Effectiveness and Measures of Performance are the raw materials for these tradeoffs.

Figure 6.1(a) *continues*

FIGURE 6.1(a) Activities needed to deliver capabilities and
requirements baseline. *(continued)*

2. Establish Baseline Requirements—Define the Measures of Performance

Perform Fact-Finding

Produce an overall statement of the problem in the operational context.
Develop the overall operational and technical objectives of the target
system through Measures of Performance (MoP) for the requirements.
Define the boundaries and interfaces of the target system.

Gather and Classify the Requirements

Gather required operational capabilities; functional, nonfunctional, and
environmental requirements; and design constraints.
Build a top-down capabilities and functional deconstruction of the
requirements in a flow-down tree using a requirements tool.

Evaluate and Rationalize Requirements

Answer the question "Why do we need this?" in terms of operational
benefits.
Build a cost/benefit model using probabilistic assessments of all variables
and dependencies.
For technical requirements, perform a risk assessment of the cost and
schedule.

Prioritize Requirements

Determine the criticality of the functions to the system's mission.
Determine tradeoff relations for all requirements to be used when option
decisions are made.
For technical items, prioritize the costs and dependencies.

Integrate and Validate Requirements

Address completeness of requirements by removing all TBD items.
Validate that requirements agree and are traceable to capabilities, goals,
and the mission.
Resolve any requirement inconsistencies and conflicts.

FIGURE 6.1(b) Activities for developing and executing the Performance Measurement Baseline.

3. Establish Performance Measurement Baseline (PMB)—Define Technical Performance Measures

Deconstruct Requirements into Work Packages and Planning Packages.

Deconstruct the program scope into a product based work breakdown structure (WBS).

Deconstruct the WBS into work packages describing the production of all deliverables and processes traceable to the requirements.

Assign Accountability for the Deliverables from Each Work Package

Assign accountability for work packages for the management of resource allocation, cost baseline, and technical delivery to a named owner.

Arrange Work Packages in a Logical Order

Arrange work packages in a network with defined deliverables, milestones, internal and external dependencies, appropriate schedule, and cost margin.

Develop the Budgeted Cost for Work Scheduled (BCWS) for Each Work Package and Planning Package

Develop a time-phased Budgeted Cost for Work Scheduled (BCWS) for labor and material costs in each work package.

Develop a time-phased Budgeted Cost for Work Scheduled (BCWS) for the program as a whole.

Ensure that proper resource allocations can be met and budget profiles match expectations of the program sponsor.

Assign Measures of Performance (MoP), Key Performance Parameters (KPP), and Technical Performance Measures (TPM)

Assign an objective Measure of Performance (MoP) for each critical work package's deliverables.

Trace critical deliverables to the Measure of Effectiveness (MoE) defined in the capabilities baseline.

Summarize these Measures of Performance (MoP) and Measures of Effectiveness (MoE) for the program as a whole.

Assign measures of physical percent complete for each work package.

Assign measures of physical percent complete for the program as a whole.

Set the Performance Measurement Baseline (PMB)

Establish a Performance Measurement Baseline (PMB) to forecast work package and project ongoing and completion cost and schedule metrics.

Figure 6.1(b) *continues*

FIGURE 6.1(b) Activities for developing and executing the Performance Measurement Baseline. *(continued)*

4. Execute the Performance Measurement Baseline (PMB)—Maintain Cost, Schedule, and Technical Performance

Perform Authorized Work in the Planned Sequence

Using the work package sequencing, release work to be performed as planned. With the RACI-based RAM, the accountable delivery manager guides the development of the products or services for each work package.

Accumulate and Report Work Package Physical Performance

Using physical percent complete or apportioned milestones, capture the measures of "progress to plan" for each work package.
Report the physical percent complete in a centralized system for each work package and the program as a whole.

Analyze Work Package Performance

Compare the actual percent complete against the planned percent complete for each period of performance.
Construct cost and schedule performance indices from this information and the physical percent complete measures.

Take Corrective Management Action for Any Variance in Work Package Performance

With the cost and schedule performance indices, construct a forecast of future performance of cost, schedule, and technical performance compliance.
Take management actions for any work packages not performing as planned.

Maintain Performance Measurement Baseline's Integrity

Record past performance based on work package completion criteria.
Record previous future performance estimates in a historical database.
Forecast future performance against the Performance Measurement Baseline.
Report the future performance estimate to the program stakeholders.

Levels of Implementation

There is a long history of tailoring processes and practices to suit the needs of the project.[1] The notion that we can select a set of practices and processes and apply them to everything that comes our way is simply poor management. For all projects, one approach to categorizing the levels of tailoring is to look at the components of the project:

> **Business Risk.** The value at risk might affect how the practices are applied.

> **Project Requirements.** These are the "ilities" of the project, like reliability, maintainability, operability, interfaceability, sustainability, compatibilities, and others are aspects of complexity, and will affect how the practices are tailored.

> **Approach to Execution.** The procurement strategy, the complexity of the deliverables, the control of cost, schedule, and technical deliverables, resource planning and management, the physical sites, and other tangible differences affect the needed outcomes practices, and will affect how the practices are applied.

We must understand not only the practices and processes but also how they effect the success of the project. Tailoring provides the ability to integrate, consolidate, incorporate, and streamline the practices and processes. This results in streamlining to the maximum extent possible, consistent with the principles of the project management activities, to deliver the needed capabilities most efficiently and effectively. To determine the level of tailoring, the project manager must decide how much practice and process is enough for the project.

The tailoring process must ensure that:

> The practices and processes deliver the project in the shortest practical time

> Risk is balanced against technical and operational outcomes

> Adequate information is provided to the decision makers

Tailoring of the Performance-Based Project Management practices and processes has three levels:

1. **Level 1: Minimal implementation of the practices.** The project is small, the desired outcomes are known, the users are identified, and they agree on the outcomes. The technology or processes are known to work. The "value at risk" is low. There is high confidence in the budget and schedule. This type of project is common in all business domains; for example, it is the type of project that adds some feature to an existing system; it upgrades or updates an existing product to service; it installs an expanded service or capability, or performs some analysis and produces a report in an area that is understood.

2. **Level 2: Moderate implementation of the practices.** The project is developing something new within a known technical or operational domain. Teams of people who have the right skills and experience but may have not worked with each other before create issues that go beyond just the technical risks.

3. **Level 3: Major implementation of the practices.** When the project is complex and risky, we must apply all of the elements of each practice to the project.

Level 1: Minimal Implementation

For minimal implementation projects, we will use a lightweight communication process as a starting point. Minimal implementation affects each of the practices.

Define Capabilities

We can define the capabilities through operational concepts by constructing a short narrative of what the system is supposed to do. This can be treated as an *elevator pitch,* with short, to-the-point descriptions that define the outcomes and benefits of each capability. These capabilities can easily be described with nouns and verbs identifying the "what" and the "how" of the capability. We can assess the needs, costs, and risks of each capability by making a list of each capability and assigning the costs and risk to each element in the list. Once we have this information, we can discover the alternatives. Any redundancies in the capabilities will become clear when we examine the capabilities side-by-side, and we can remove them by combining or eliminating the capability.

Establish the Requirements Baseline

A simple list of the requirements will work here. This list can be a few sentences for each requirement, with each one connected to a capability to ensure that the reader understands that both—not just the requirement, but also the capability that will support the business strategy—are needed. Once the list of requirements is complete, we can start to partition them into classes for further assessment by the stakeholders, who can confirm the need, see the connection to the capability, and agree that each requirement should move forward to the planning, scheduling, and budgeting step. For example there may be technical performance requirements—throughput, size, weight, power capacity. Or human interface requirements—fit to a person's hand, desirable colors for a car, or readability of text size on a display. These classes of requirements can then be grouped and assessed together for impacts on cost, schedule, and risk.

The activities for the minimal requirements implementation are:

> Prioritize a list of requirements containing a short narrative with the project's participants. This should be done in a face-to-face manner.

> Name the person accountable for each requirement and ensure that there are sufficient resources to deliver the solution to the requirement.

> Connect a capability to the requirement that it supports through the list of requirements, so the project participants can confirm that all the capabilities are being developed through the requirements.

Establish the Performance Measurement Baseline

The Performance Measurement Baseline can be a simple cost and schedule worksheet describing what work will be performed, the budget for that work, and the name of the person accountable for producing the outcomes of the work.

The activities for the minimal PMB develop are:

> List the outcomes of the project.

> Assign a person responsible for producing those outcomes.

> Create a schedule showing when the outcomes will be delivered. This schedule can be notional, meaning informal. No need to put together a fancy schedule using a scheduling tool. A drawing on the whiteboard or sticky notes on the wall will do—anything that shows the order of the work and the order of the outcomes.

> Create a top-level budget for all the work to be performed.

> Create a defined way of measuring progress to plan. The simplest is to count the features, requirements, and capabilities and use percent complete.

> Set the baseline for the project so everyone knows what "done" looks like for the planned work. Maintain this baseline by updating the whiteboard or sticky notes and recording the current date somewhere visible.

Execute the Performance Measurement Baseline

With the capabilities understood, the requirements defined for those capabilities, the schedule in place, the people assigned, and the budget committed, it is time to start executing the project. The project participants should know what they are assigned to do, so executing the work means doing the planned work in the planned order.

The activities for the minimal PMB execution are:

> Look at the sequence of the planned work and do it. In the agile world, or in this minimal implementation where sticky notes are

used, take the note from the planned column and move it to the "doing work" column. It's really that easy.

> With the work under way, record the actual costs. This includes labor and materials. This can be done using a simple spreadsheet, but it is important to capture these costs in order to tell if we're on budget or not.

> For the work performed at the cost absorbed, look at the outcomes and confirm they meet the agreed-upon specifications. The simplest way for this to happen is to ask the user of the features, products, or services if they agree we are "done."

> When there are gaps, bring everyone together and determine the next steps to put things right.

> The project manager is accountable for the overall performance of the project, and, where implementation is minimal, the project manager is likely directly engaged in hands-on oversight of the project's activities.

Perform Continuous Risk Management

Risks are prevalent in all projects, even in small projects. Managing risk is the primary role of project management. No matter the size or complexity of the project, we need to address risks up front and apply Continuous Risk Management throughout the project's life cycle. Remember that risk comes from uncertainty, so start by answering the question, "What are we uncertain about?" Write the answers down and post them on the wall. Our five steps in Continuous Risk Management for the minimal application are:

1. **Identify.** Make a list, post it on the wall, have the team stand in front of this list and confirm these are the things that need to be addressed.

2. **Analyze.** For each of the risks, determine the impact on the project and the overall project outcome and devise a handling strategy.

3. **Plan.** Make a plan for how to handle the risk. This means discussing with the team what to do about the technical, cost, and

schedule impacts should the risk occur. Or better, what actions can be taken to reduce the uncertainty associated with the risk and/or to make it go away.

4. **Track.** Report on the progress of the risk-handling activities periodically in the same way you report on the progress of the features and functions being developed. This periodic risk assessment cycle is why it is called "Continuous" Risk Management.

5. **Control.** As the risks become issues, or the risk-reduction activities don't produce the desired results, deal with them as they occur. Don't wait. As Colin Powell and others have said, "Bad news is not like wine. It doesn't improve with age."

Level 2: Moderate Implementation

Projects with moderate implementation needs usually have a project team, a customer, and a written set of needs and requirements. The complexity of such a project can involve something new, something created from an existing system, or a different business domain, or different technology, where what to do is not as obvious as it is in a project requiring minimal implementation. It involves more communication and more risks, and it is more difficult to discover what "done" looks like. It may include distributed teams and customers who may not be in the same room or as easily accessible.

Define Capabilities

We need to define the capabilities in a form that matches the business case and the vocabulary of the business or mission sponsors. This starts with Concept of Operations (ConOps), a Statement of Objectives (SOO), or a Statement of Work (SOW) that uses the language of the buyer. These documents, whichever one is chosen, provide traceability of the project's needs in some hierarchical structure so the user of the resulting system can see how the capabilities are related to each other. This can be done using a "tree" structure, where each top-level capability has "children" (the lower-level capabilities) that support it. This approach is the foundation for a more formal requirements elicitation process, as we'll see next. The key here is to provide a narrative that everyone can agree on and understand. This narrative describes what "done" looks like in units of measure meaningful to the decision makers.

Establish the Requirements Baseline

Requirements at the moderate level need to be stated in more detail than those at a minimal level. This means we need measures of performance that can be assessed during development and confirmed by the users when the system is delivered. A simple form of "requirements management" can be used. This can be a list, with the attributes of the requirements. It needs to include the priorities, of course, but more important, this list needs confirmable connection to the capabilities. The confirmation process ensures that there is no redundancy, duplication, or gaps and that each requirement is stand-alone. The fancy term for this is *Mutually Exclusive and Collectively Exhaustive (MECE).*[2] This means there are no overlaps and no gaps in the requirements. *No overlaps* means the requirements are grouped so that there is no "double counting" of the requirement. *No gaps* means all the requirements taken together cover all the possible options for the project's capabilities. This helps ensure that nothing was overlooked when developing the requirements from the list of capabilities.

The activities for moderate implementation of the requirements baseline include the following:

> ➤ Manage the requirements in a way that connects the dots between the capabilities of the technical and operational requirements.

> ➤ Make further partitions on the list of requirements to reveal how they are coupled and how cohesive they are.

> ➤ Capture the requirements and put them where everyone can look at them and comment on them. You can use simple notes on the wall, a spreadsheet, or a database.

> ➤ Assign a business value to each requirement. This will help answer the question, "Why do we need this?" and allow us to assess the impact of the requirement if we decide not to deliver it.

> Connect the requirements to an assessment of their cost to develop and the schedule for that development. We can't make a credible assessment of a requirement's worth without knowing its cost and schedule impact on the project.

Establish the Performance Measurement Baseline

With the capabilities defined and the requirements that will implement those capabilities identified, we need to develop the schedule and cost for the work needed to produce the outcomes from the project. We've developed the connections between capabilities and the requirements. In moderate implementation, we will use the notion of a work package. These are the activities for the moderate implementation needed to complete the Performance Measurement Baseline:

> Deconstruct the work into work packages, each of which produces only a single tangible outcome with a measure of physical percent complete attached to it. If this measure is a performance measure, it needs to be a technical performance measure. How fast, how high, how reliable, how much does it weigh, and how much capacity are all measures of performance. Define something that the customer can look at and say, "Yep, that's what I wanted."

> Build a formal Responsibility Assignment Matrix (RAM) for the major deliverables of the project, which clearly and concisely states "who" is accountable for producing the outcomes. Although the name of the matrix includes the word *responsible,* the matrix also includes *accountable, consulted,* and *informed,* which together with *responsible* are known as RACI.[3] Make the connection to the person accountable and the other three will follow.

> Arrange the work packages in the order that produces the best value to the customers—the order that allows the customers to receive the needed capabilities in the order of priority, so they can put these capabilities to work. The customer gets to say what this order is, not the project team. There are constraints, of course, with the physical limitations. No installing the carpet before the painting is done. But the customers have the final say, since it is their money.

➤ Assign the budget for the total project to the individual account-able for performing the work using your RAM. This moves the accountability down from the project manager to those actually performing the work. They should be able to determine how to best spend this budget. Without this transfer, those doing the work become simply labor.

➤ Measure the performance of each work package. Since the work package has a single outcome, we can assign some tangible measure of compliance to the requirement and its support of the capability. Write this down, use it in the conversations with the person accountable, and always use it as the basis for measuring progress toward "done." The passage of time and consumption of time and money is never a measure of progress.

➤ "Baseline" this information. Do this once you collect the work packages, the requirements, who is accountable for delivering the requirements, the sequence of the work packages, and the assigned budget for each work package. The primary purpose for baselining this—or anything, for that matter—is that we can't manage a project without knowing the variances in our performance. We can't determine variances if we don't have something to compare our current status to, and that is the baseline.

Execute the Performance Measurement Baseline

Now that we have the work packages, the assigned people, a budget, and a schedule, and we know what "done" looks like for each outcome of the project in units meaningful to the decision makers, it is time to actually do the work.

Albert Einstein once asked, "What is the purpose of time?" The an-swer is, "Time keeps everything from happening at once." The order of execution is defined in the Integrated Master Schedule (IMS). It is called "integrated" because it contains everything we need to manage the project—cost, schedule, assigned resources, descriptions of the out-comes, and measures of performance. It is a single place to look to see what "done" looks like.

Executing the Performance Measurement Baseline means:

> **Performing the authorized work in the planned order.** When there is a need to perform the work out of order, assess the impact on the overall project's cost and schedule.

> **Maintaining the budget performance to plan at the work package (WP) level.** Keeping on budget at the lowest level of the project prevents the accumulation of poor budget performance from leaking into other work packages.

> **Examining the cost and schedule performance at the WP level.** By focusing your management efforts lower down in the project plan, you can also prevent leakage into other portions of the projects. Also, focusing on the work efforts that produce the tangible outcomes provides insight into what is actually happening rather than just a summary of performance that many times hides the details.

> **Taking managerial action at the WP level to correct cost, schedule, and technical performance issues before they leak into other parts of the project.** A phrase to remember is "keep it GREEN." That way you'll never have a RED and rarely a YELLOW condition.

> **Maintaining the overall cost and performance schedule for which the project manager is accountable.** The WP managers are accountable for their individual work packages. This relationship between the project manager and the work package managers separates the concerns of the project's participants.[4]

Perform Continuous Risk Management

Like our minimal project, risk is present here as well—only more so. The same five steps for managing this risk are applied:

1. **Identify.** Develop a list of risks at the WP level and review it during the periodic project performance meetings. Focus at the WP level, so coupling can be minimized and cohesion maximized[5] The assignment of risk to the work package starts at the project level with the work breakdown structure (WBS). The terminal

nodes of the WBS are usually the work packages performing the work, so this is a natural process of "flowing down" risk to the location of the work.

2. **Analyze.** Determine the impact of each risk on the outcome at the WP level and provide one of the four handling strategies: (1) *Risk Avoidance*, which includes not performing an activity that could carry risk; (2) *Risk Reduction*, which involves reducing the severity of the loss or the likelihood of the loss from occurring; (3) *Sharing*, which involves sharing with another party the burden of loss or the benefit of gain that results from a risk, and the measures to reduce a risk; and (4) *Retention*, which involves accepting the loss or benefit of a risk when it occurs.

3. **Plan.** The project manager guides the risk-handling processes using the activities illustrated in Figure 3.3.

4. **Track.** Tracking these processes can be achieved by monitoring the residual risk to determine the potential impact on the project. As the risk-handling processes are executed, the risk should be reduced and the residual risk reduced as well. Once this residual risk reaches some agreed-on level, the risk can be considered "under control." The actual measurement is highly project dependent, so continuous review of the risk, its reduction, and the remaining risk value is part of the periodic conversation with the customer.

5. **Control.** The risks can be controlled by performing the handling processes to address the emerging risk impact and the resulting residual risk.

Level 3: Major Implementation

In Level 3 projects, we have more at risk, more complexity, more technology, more of everything. Level 3 projects require more formality. It is likely many of the participants in the project are not directly accessible to the project team. In the modern enterprise, locations may be spread around the world. Also, people working in these large and distributed organizations have day jobs and cannot be easily dedicated to the project or easily respond to a set of questions. The first solution to this situation—it can't be a problem, since that is the way things work—is to manage the project through a set of formal process and practices, based on documentation. This documentation-centric project management paradigm is our "major" project management approach.

Define Capabilities

We can now apply more formal capabilities development processes. Capabilities start with the mission level analysis of what "done" looks like. These capabilities needed to be developed through a formal process shown in Figure 6.2. This process starts with the needs of the customer. The priorities of these needs are documented through a selection process and scenarios describing the capabilities. The capabilities are partitioned into *classes*—technology, operations, customer facing, internal, maintenance, and so on—so we can sort them out later. The future environment is added to ensure that we are not building an "instant legacy" system. The capabilities are assembled into a *capabilities goal*.

The operational concepts described through scenarios or use cases provide insight into the assessment of these concepts compared to the current planned capabilities. Any mismatches are revealed so they can be closed. From this process, we are able to define the "solution space" for our capabilities, and with it we can start asking questions about the return on our investment in the capabilities—when we earn back our money if we possess this capability. This can be answered using a balancing process among our resources, the mission or business case priorities, and the "affordability" plan for producing the capability.

Establish the Requirements Baseline

In large, complex systems, there are two fundamental classes of requirements—process performance requirements and product performance requirements. Figure 6.3 shows how these are related. Our requirements elicitation process must separate these if it is to have any

FIGURE 6.2 Formal process for identifying capabilities.

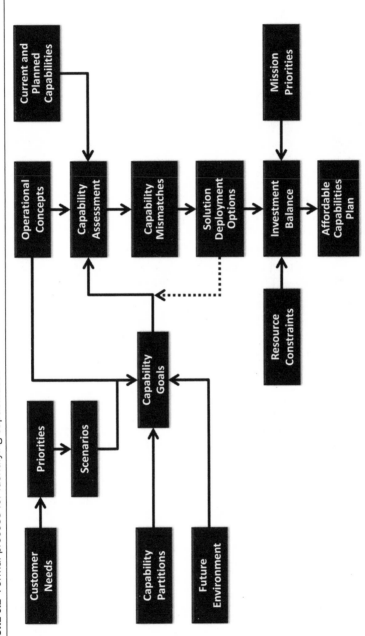

Source: Abstracted from "Capabilities-Based Planning — How It Is Intended To Work and Challenges to Its Successful Implementation," Col. Stephen K. Walker, United States Army, U. S. Army War College, March 2005.

FIGURE 6.3 Process and product performance requirements.

Enterprise Mission Statement	Process Functional Requirements	Process Interface Requirements	Process Specialty Requirements	Process Environment Requirements
		Process Performance Requirements		SOW & Plans

Customer Need Statement	Product Functional Requirements	Product Interface Requirements	Product Specialty Requirements	Product Environment Requirements
		Product Performance Requirements		Specifications

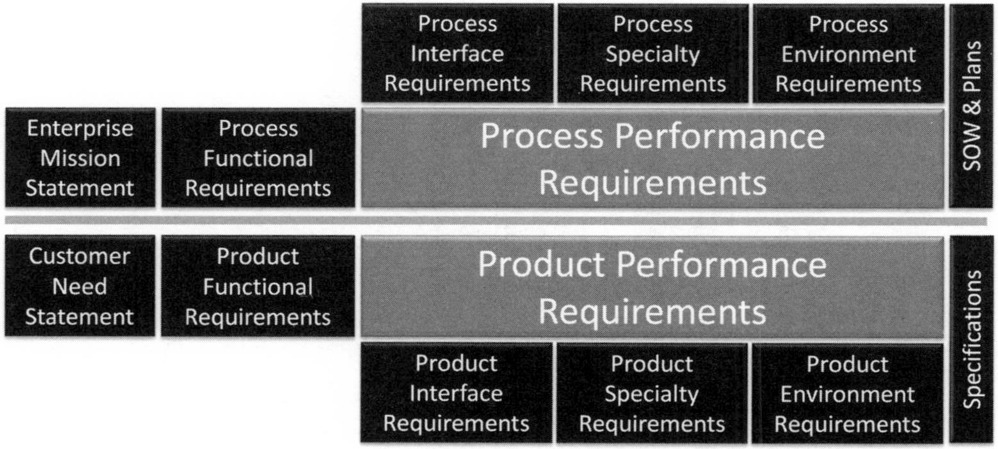

SOURCE: *Systems Requirements Analysis*, Jeffrey O. Grady, McGraw Hill, 1993

integrity. Mixing them creates confusion about what is important for products and what is important for processes.

> ➤ Process performance requirements define what the system must do when it is complete and how well it must do those things from the point of view of the customer's business or mission needs.

> ➤ Product performance requirements define how the system must behave at the product level, while fulfilling the process performance requirements.

Establish the Performance Measurement Baseline

With the process and product requirements in place, we can start to build the Performance Measurement Baseline. As shown in Figure 6.4, the PMB has three baselines:

> ➤ The Technical Performance Baseline is the requirements flow-down and traceability map for each deliverable in the program. A critical performance measure of the Technical Performance Baseline is the stability of requirements. The expected technical achievement for the actual progress is compared using periodic measurements or test starts against the Technical Performance Baseline. An important function of the Technical Performance Baseline is to define the units of measurement for each deliverable in order to define what "done" looks like at each incremental assessment of maturity.

> ➤ The Schedule Performance Baseline is the sequence of work packages and planning packages that produce the products or services to be generated by the project.

> ➤ The Cost Performance Baseline is the "authorized time–phased budget used to measure, monitor, and control overall cost performance on the program." This budget (BCWS) is held in the control accounts, the work packages and planning packages owned by the work package managers.

FIGURE 6.4 The Performance Measurement Baseline has three baselines.

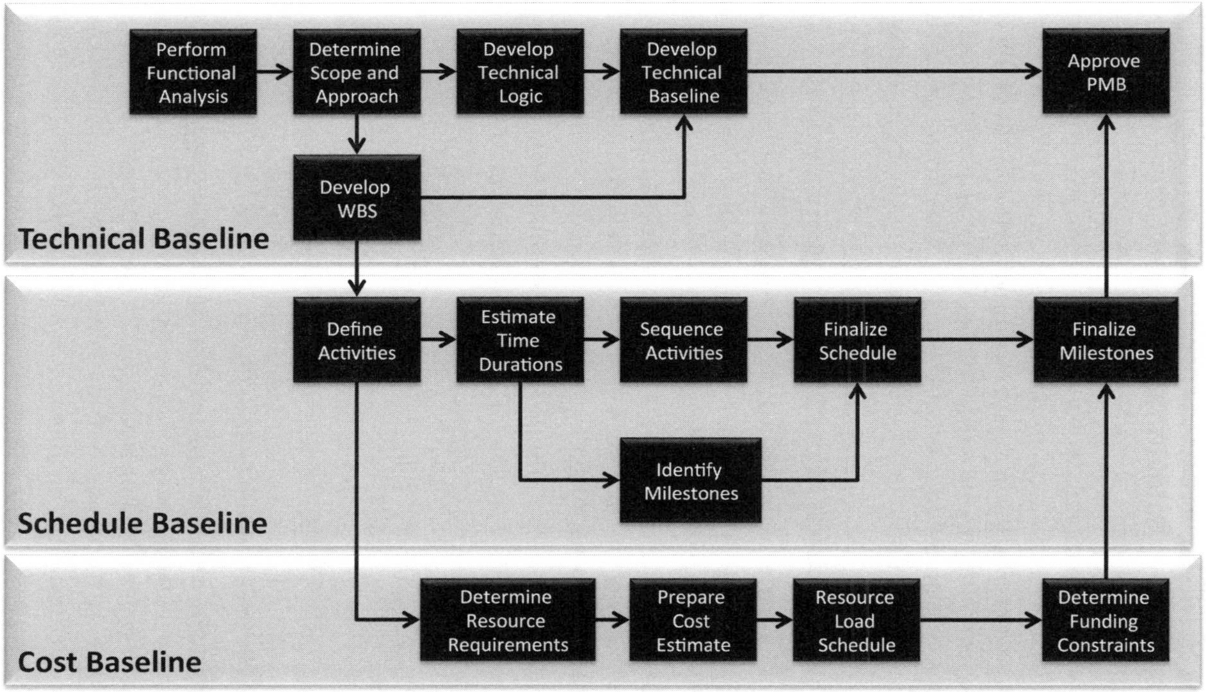

Execute the Performance Measurement Baseline

With the baseline established, we now need to execute it in a manner that increases the probability of project success. There are five steps in this execution process:

1. Authorize and perform the work according to the plan described in the network of work packages held in a scheduling tool. The formality of using a scheduling tool provides both control and visibility for managing the authorized work. The schedule shows when work is planned to start and complete. The project manager can use this to confirm work is being performed in the agreed order.

2. Accumulate and report performance data about cost and physical percent complete for the deliverables from the work packages.

3. Analyze the performance data derived from the performance metrics and make any adjustments to the network of work packages.

4. Take management actions for any variances to ensure on-time, on-budget, and on-specification of all deliverables produced by the work packages.

5. Maintain the Performance Management Baseline throughout the program's duration for all earned value parameters.

These five steps are repeated periodically throughout the life of the project. They are the *business rhythm* of the project management process.

Perform Continuous Risk Management

Our Continuous Risk Management process for the major implementation uses the same framework as the other two implementations. This is shown in more detail in Figure 6.5. These processes are applied in greater detail in the major implementation than in the others, but we still must identify, analyze, plan, track, and control the risks as well as communicate everything we are doing about risk management to all the stakeholders.

FIGURE 6.5 Continuous Risk Management process.

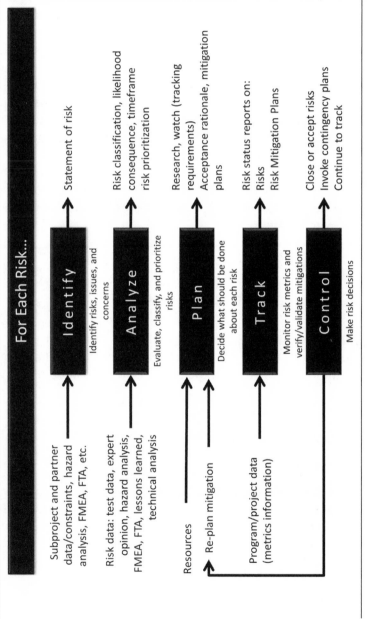

Looking Back

With the three tailored project paradigms, we can see the principles are always the same, the practices are adjusted to provide the appropriate level of detail needed to manage the project, and the processes are tailored to fit the needs of the project's planning, cost, resource management, reporting, and risk management needs. Figures 6.2 through 6.5 summarize the practices of Performance-Based Project Management. These practices can be tailored in a variety of ways but must always adhere to the principles and processes. Tailoring the practices starts with the question, "What is the value at risk?" The answer to this will lead you to consider how much detail to apply. If the value at risk is small, then tailor the practices in a small way. If the value at risk is large, then take appropriate actions to ensure that value is protected with the proper practice implementation.

What's Ahead?

In Chapter 7, we will see what elements need to be in place for Performance-Based Project Management to succeed. Like the tailored practices, these components can be tailored, but at minimum they will include:

> The Statement of Work
> The Integrated Master Schedule
> The Risk Management Plan
> A staffing plan
> A testing plan
> A delivery plan

CHAPTER 7

Deliverables Needed for Project Management Success

Performance-Based Project Management produces tangible documents that are evidence that the method has been used. These documents are in addition to the contracts and other program documents normally found in a large, complex systems development effort. The documents and evidence they represent are materials produced during the project that demonstrate the increasing maturity of the products or services. Although these alone are not measures of progress, they are the supporting materials for these measures. The documentation for each deliverable becomes part of a larger set of documents needed to give the customer visibility into the performance of the project. Ultimately, the working products or services are the tangible evidence of progress to plan.

The documents start with the Statement of Work (SOW), which describes the deliverables from the project. The SOW contains a narrative of the work to be performed on the project. This is an anchor usually provided by the customer, but it may also be developed jointly by the customer and the provider of the products or services of the project. In all cases, a well-written SOW lays the groundwork for success of the project.

Documents Needed During the Execution of a Project

Some in the project management business say that Performance-Based Project Management requires too many documents or that the documents are too complex. This approach uses documents as a narrative between the requesters of the project's outcomes and the providers of those outcomes. The physical nature of each document is not defined; only that they are needed and must contain a minimal set of information that the customer and provider can use to take action or make decisions.

Most of these documents have been introduced in previous chapters. In this chapter, we will develop the details needed for the following documents so that you can actually produce them for your own projects:

> **Statement of Work (SOW).** Establishes and defines all nonspecification requirements for the work efforts of the project.

> **Statement of Objectives (SOO).** States the overall performance objectives.

> **Concept of Operations (ConOps).** A verbal or graphic statement that clearly and concisely expresses what the customer intends to accomplish and how it will be done using available resources.

> **Work breakdown structure (WBS).** A product-oriented family tree of hardware, software, services, data, and facilities that are required for system development, deployment, and sustainment.

> **Organizational breakdown structure (OBS).** The hierarchical description of the staff that works on the project.

> **Responsibility Assignment Matrix (RAM).** The intersection of the WBS and the OBS, showing "who" is doing "what" work to produce the outcomes from the project.

> **Integrated Master Schedule (IMS).** An integrated, networked schedule containing all the detailed discrete work packages and planning packages necessary to accomplish the project.

> **Risk Management Plan (RMP).** A plan to foresee risks, estimate impacts, and define responses to issues.

> **Performance Measurement Baseline (PMB).** A time-phased budget plan for accomplishing work, against which contract performance is measured. It includes the budgets assigned to scheduled control accounts and the applicable indirect budgets.

> **Requirements Traceability Matrix (RTM).** A tool used to ensure that the project's scope, requirements, and deliverables are connected with each other.

> **Measures of Effectiveness (MoE).** Operational measures of success that are closely related to the achievements of the mission or operational objectives evaluated in the operational environment under a specific set of conditions.

> **Measures of Performance (MoP).** Measures that characterize physical or functional attributes relating to the system operation, measured or estimated under specific conditions.

> **Key Performance Parameters (KPP).** Capabilities and characteristics so significant that failure to meet them can be cause for reevaluation, reassessment, or termination of the program.

> **Technical Performance Measures (TPM).** Attributes that determine how well a system or system element is satisfying or expected to satisfy a technical requirement or goal.

Statement of Work

The Statement of Work is the start of the project. It is a document developed by the customer, sometimes with the help of the supplier of the products or services, but written primarily from the customer's point of view. The SOW, as its name suggests, describes the work to be performed during the project that will produce the project's outcomes. The term *work* is broad. It could mean buying something, teaming up with someone to provide the solution, installing a "ready-made" solution, or actually building something, although that is not always necessary.

The SOW specifies in clear and understandable language the work to be done in producing the outcomes of the project through the delivered products or services. An effective SOW requires both an understanding of the goods or services that are needed to satisfy a particular requirement and an ability to define what is required in specific, performance-based, quantitative terms. This sounds like a lot of work, but the SOW is the core document for the success of any project. It enables suppliers to clearly understand the customer's needs. This allows the suppliers to prepare a credible proposal to deliver the required goods or services.

The SOW must state the requirements in general terms of what (result) is to be done, rather than how (method) it is done. It gives the supplier the maximum flexibility to devise the best method to accomplish the required result. However, the SOW must also be descriptive and specific enough to protect the interests of the customer and to promote competition between multiple suppliers. The clarity and explicitness of the requirements in the SOW will enhance the quality of the proposals submitted. A definitive SOW is the source of definitive proposals, which reduces the time needed for proposal evaluation.

Preparing a Statement of Work begins with an analytical process that involves an examination of the customer's requirements and tends to be a "bottom-up" assessment with "reengineering" potential. Each requirement needs to be connected to a capability the customer is asking for. When we start at the bottom and work our way up, we may have requirements that have no home—no capability to support. One of two things can be done. Drop the requirement or reassess a possible missing capability. When we start the Statement of Work at the top and work down, we have no way to determine if we have missed any requirements that may be needed from missing or undiscovered capabilities. This analysis is the basis for establishing performance requirements, developing performance standards, writing the performance work statement, and producing the quality assurance plan. Those responsible for the mission or program are essential to the writing of the SOW and defining the needed capabilities produced by the project.

A SOW describes the work to be performed and usually includes a timeline and level of effort so that a vendor or contractor can respond to the Request for Quote (RFQ) with a proposal and cost estimate. The customer can then select the most qualified vendor at the most affordable cost.

SOWs should include:

> Work to be performed and location of the work to demonstrate how the job will be completed as planned

> Period of performance, timeline, and deliverable schedule

> Any special requirements

The evaluation criteria may include the bidder's:

> Plan for performing the work described in the SOW. This plan may or may not be a full schedule, but the sequence of the work and the identified outcomes need to be described. A partial schedule can be developed for the upcoming work in enough detail to manage the project. For work beyond the planning horizon, a budget and a general description of what will be done is called "rolling wave" planning.

> Skill and experience of the individuals who will perform the work and their assigned work efforts.

> Past performance and completed projects to demonstrate competency, capability, and capacity to perform the work correctly.

> Price of the proposed products or services.

Statement of Objectives

The Statement of Objectives is an alternative to a Statement of Work. The SOO is a broader description of the outcomes of the project used when the technical and operational details are not needed to convey what "done" looks like to those implementing the project. It is a summary of key goals, outcomes, or both, which is incorporated into performance-based contracts so that competitors can propose their solutions, including their technical approach, performance standards, and a quality assurance surveillance plan based on commercial business practices.

The SOO should not address each WBS element, but each WBS element should be traceable to and do something included in the SOO. For example, a SOO may instruct the bidder to address the engineering approach. That is not a particular WBS element, but several WBS elements might be created to break out the engineering tasks. Try not to group all WBS elements in the same objective. End users will get the best service, and competition will be maintained, if dissimilar objectives are submitted to contractors on separate SOOs.

The Statement of Objectives provides basic, top-level objectives of the project and is provided in the Request for Proposal (RFP) in lieu of a formal Statement of Work. The SOO gives potential suppliers the flexibility to develop cost-effective solutions and the opportunity to propose innovative alternatives meeting the objectives.

Concept of Operations

A Concept of Operations (ConOps) describes from the user's perspective a system's characteristics, the needed capabilities it will fulfill, its relationship to other systems, and the ways it will be used. A ConOps can also describe the user's organization, mission, and objectives from an integrated systems point of view and is used to communicate overall quantitative and qualitative system characteristics to stakeholders. It describes the characteristics of a proposed system from the viewpoint of those who will use that system. The ConOps includes:

> ➤ Statement of the goals and objectives of the system assessed through Measures of Effectiveness (MoE).

> ➤ The current system or situation with background, objectives, and scope. The operational policies and constraints in the current system. This description should identify the operational environment and its characteristics, the major components of the system and the interconnections between these components, the interfaces to external systems, and the capabilities and functions of the current system.

> ➤ Strategies, tactics, policies, and constraints affecting the system.

> ➤ Organizations, activities, and interactions among participants and stakeholders.

> ➤ Clear statement of responsibilities and authorities delegated.

> ➤ Specific operational processes for fielding the system.

> ➤ Processes for initiating, developing, maintaining, and retiring the system.

A ConOps should relate a narrative of the process to be followed in implementing a system. It should define the roles of the stakeholders involved throughout the process. The ConOps should provide a clear methodology to realize the goals and objectives of the system, but it should not be an implementation or transition plan itself.

A typical ConOps table of contents looks like this:

> ➤ Key goals of the resulting system

> ➤ Key assumptions in achieving those goals

> ➤ Stated purpose of the ConOps

> ➤ Major business functions or major mission functions

> ➤ Entities performing these functions

> ➤ Major supporting technology

> ➤ New capabilities' effect on managing the business or leading the mission

> ➤ Top-level schedule for deploying the needed capabilities

Work Breakdown Structure

A formal definition of a project work breakdown structure "is a deliverable or product-oriented grouping of project work elements shown in graphical display to organize and subdivide the total work scope of a project."[1] The WBS is a critically important project tool for the simple reason that it is the first place the actual deliverables of the project are listed and their behaviors named in the WBS dictionary. The WBS dictionary describes the technical and operational measures needed to confirm that the deliverable from the WBS has been correctly implemented. This narrative, often referred to as a "build to specification," describes the "acceptable criteria" for the deliverable. Thought and planning must be given to the development and implementation of the WBS and the accompanying dictionary so that the need for subsequent changes is minimized.

This WBS framework, as illustrated in Figure 4.3, allows the project to be separated into its logical component parts and makes the relationship of the parts clear. It defines the project in terms of hierarchically related action-oriented elements. Each element provides logical summary points for assessing technical accomplishments and for measuring cost and schedule performance.

WBS Development

A work breakdown structure is the foundation for effective project planning, execution, controlling, statusing, and reporting. All the work contained in the WBS is to be identified, estimated, scheduled, and budgeted using the WBS number. The WBS is the hierarchical structure and a set of codes that integrates project deliverables, from the lowest work element to the final system deliverable—the delivered capabilities. The WBS contains the project's scope baseline that is used to achieve the technical objectives of the project. The WBS is generally a multilevel framework that organizes and graphically displays elements representing work to be accomplished in logical relationships.[2]

The project manager structures the project work into WBS elements (work packages) that are:[3]

> **Definable.** The deliverables of the project can be described and easily understood by project participants.

> **Manageable.** The size and complexity of the work can be assigned to people with specific responsibility and authority.

> **Estimable.** The duration and effort of the work can be estimated with confidence, along with the cost and the resources required to complete the work as planned.

> **Independent.** Each element of the WBS has a minimum interface with or dependence on other elements.

> **Integrable.** Each element of work can be integrated with other project work elements and with higher-level cost estimates and schedules to include the overall project.

> **Measurable.** Each element of work has a means to measure progress. The work has start and completion dates and measurable interim milestones.

> **Adaptable.** Each work element is sufficiently flexible so the addition, change, or elimination of work scope can be accommodated in the WBS framework.

WBS Dictionary

Relationships between the WBS elements and detailed descriptions of each element are presented in the WBS dictionary that accompanies the hierarchical WBS diagram. The WBS dictionary is a project definition tool that defines the scope for each work element; documents the assumptions about the work, including deliverables, milestones, key performance parameters, and quantities; lists required resources and processes to accomplish the work; identifies a completion schedule, including measurable milestones; and provides links to key technical design or engineering documents.

A WBS dictionary is a set of specific definitions that thoroughly describes the scope of each work element identified in the WBS. It defines each WBS element down to the control account or work package level in terms of the content of the work to be performed. The dictionary is composed of two components:

> ➤ A tabular summary of the dictionary elements cross-referenced to the WBS indenture level, the WBS revision, the element title, the project contractor WBS code, and (if desired) the contractor's accounting code.

> ➤ A work element dictionary sheet that provides the title of the work element, the project contractor WBS and the contractor's accounting codes, the budget and reporting number, and a detailed description of the work to be performed by this element, including deliverables.[4]

The WBS defines the project's deliverables and groups these project elements so that the project's work activities can be managed effectively. The OBS, defined next, shows how the staff is structured to perform this work. The WBS is product centric, not organization centric. It does not include such functions as "design" or "test." These are not deliverables from the project. Rather they are "functions" performed during the delivery of the products or services from the project. Our primary motivation for using the WBS is that it:

> ➤ Provides a framework for organizing and managing the approved project scope

> ➤ Ensures that we have defined all the work that makes up the project

> ➤ Provides a framework for planning and controlling cost and schedule information

Organizational Breakdown Structure

The organizational breakdown structure describes the structure of the workforce that delivers the products and services described in the work breakdown structure. A concise description of the OBS can be found in government documents, where the OBS is a formal document submitted monthly to the contracting officer. Through the WBS, work is defined to a level where unique organizational and personal responsibilities can be established. This may occur at any one of several levels within the project and functional organization. The individual assigned responsibility for accomplishing work at the control account level is often designated a control account manager. Control accounts are divided into smaller, discrete scopes of work called work packages, and a work package manager is assigned to each work package. Integrating the WBS with the project and functional organizations ensures that all contract work is accounted for, and that each element of work is assigned to the level of responsibility necessary for planning, tracking progress, accumulating costs, and reporting.[5]

The development of the organizational breakdown structure starts with the *organization chart.* This seems obvious, but without knowing "who" actually works on the project, we can't really arrange those resources in a way that ensures that we have enough capacity to do the work (see Figure 4.4). This organization chart also identifies the needed resources. This can be done through a skills assessment, via experience with technology or processes, or simply by using the "job titles" or "job classifications" for the available staff. Matching this structure against the elements of the work breakdown structure creates an intersection between "what has to be delivered" and "who has to deliver these outcomes." The OBS indicates the organizational relationships between the resources providing the work and the assignment of these resources to the actual work.

Responsibility Assignment Matrix

The intersection of the work breakdown structure, which shows the project's deliverables, and the organizational breakdown structure, which shows the resources assigned to produce those deliverables, is found in the Responsibility Assignment Matrix (RAM). This document may seem unnecessary for many projects, and, for smaller projects, this might be true. When someone asks, "Who is working on what?" the answer can be found in the OBS, but the RAM displays only the lowest level at which the WBS and the OBS intersect, and identifies the specific responsibilities for specific project work. At this intersection, the budget is assigned to the resources performing the work so they may produce the outcomes of that work, as shown in Figure 4.4.

With the WBS, OBS, and RAM, we have all we need to know about the "who" and "what" of our project:

> ➢ The work breakdown structure is a tool that defines a project and groups the project's elements in a way that helps organize and define the total scope of the work to be accomplished. This is done by identifying the final products and the major deliverables of the project, incorporating the appropriate levels of detail to show how the products are "assembled" for final delivery, and obtaining stakeholder agreement that these products (or services) properly represent the Statement of Work. This last piece is a narrative document—the WBS dictionary—describing the attributes of each deliverable using Measures of Effectiveness, Measures of Performance, and Technical Performance Measures.

> ➢ The OBS indicates the relationships among parts of the organization; it is used as the framework for assigning work responsibilities.

> ➢ The Responsibility Assignment Matrix merges the WBS and OBS to identify who has specific responsibility for specific project tasks shown in Figure 7.1.

Integrated Master Schedule

The Integrated Master Schedule (IMS) is a time-based network of detailed tasks necessary to ensure successful program/contract execution. The IMS is traceable to the Integrated Master Plan, the contract WBS, and the Statement of Work. The IMS is used to verify how attainable the contract objectives are, to evaluate progress toward meeting program objectives, and to coordinate the scheduled activities with all related components. Figure 4.5 illustrates how the elements of the IMS are arranged using work packages that contain the work activities needed to produce the deliverables described in the WBS and the staff described

FIGURE 7.1 Responsibility Assignment Matrix.

WBS Element	Architect / Designer			Contractor		
	Jones	Smith	Wright	Williams	Nelson	Burns
1.1 Appliances	A	R	R	A		
1.2 Cabinets	C	A			A	
1.3 Electrical	R	I				A
1.4 Plumbing	I	C	A			A

OBS Element

R – Responsible
A – Accountable
C – Consulted
I – Informed

in the OBS, who deliver the outcomes described in the SOW that fulfill the customer's needed capabilities.

Attributes of the Integrated Master Schedule

There are five core attributes of a credible Integrated Master Schedule. These attributes must be in place before the project can be considered "ready to execute." The IMS must be:

1. **Complete.** It must contain the entire project's scope of work. The WBS and its coding are included in the IMS. This means all the work activities in the IMS must be coded with the WBS number. This tells the reader "why" the work is being done, "what" is being produced, and "when" the work will produce the outcome contained in the WBS.

2. **Traceable.** This is an extension of completeness. The work in the IMS must tie into the requirements as well as the Statement of Work, Statement of Operations, and the Concept of Operations. The IMS does this by using the same numbers for each work activity as are used in these other documents.

3. **Transparent.** This is a comprehensive description of what work needs to performed, how the work will be performed, what measures of progress to plan are needed for the work, what risks are associated with the work, and the measures of performance for the outcomes from the work. By *transparent* we mean the work is "clear and concise" so there is no confusion about the outcomes or what "done" looks like.

4. **Usable.** The IMS must be used daily to execute the project. The project's participants must use it in their conversations about the status of the project, risks that are impeding progress, and who is working on what. The IMS is the "playbook" for the project. To be "usable," the IMS has to state not only what "done" looks like but also how the team is going to reach "done."

5. **Controlled.** As a critical document, the IMS must be under change control of a single responsible person. This person is the "scheduler." It is the guiding roadmap and as such must represent the current and approved directions for the project.

Four Common Mistakes in Developing and Implementing the IMS

Many projects build an Integrated Master Schedule and call it complete, without considering "how" and "why" they are producing this critical document. They simply lay out the work in some sequence, assign the work, and assume that the IMS is ready to be used to manage the project. However, if we expect to increase our project's probability of success, the following mistakes must be avoided:

> **Not aligning the IMS with the customer's needed capabilities.** The IMS must show how each of the capabilities will be developed and deployed through the work activities. This requires that the IMS be a "narrative" of these capabilities, not just a description of the work efforts. This narrative starts with work activities containing the nouns and verbs connecting the activity to the capabilities. For example, "Develop transaction processes for provider network" is a work activity supporting a

needed capability of the health insurance IT project developed in Chapter 5.

> **Not including the entire scope and the "exit criteria" for the work being performed.** "Test" is not a credible description of a work activity; but "Test database update service for provider network" is a credible description of the work. The "exit criteria" for this activity would then be contained in the WBS dictionary. These criteria are the Measures of Performance and Technical Performance Measures, and, often, the Key Performance Parameters of the deliverable produced by the work effort. The details of these are described in Chapter 3's endnotes.

> **Not cross-referencing the IMS to the project's other documents.** For example, the deliverables described in the Statement of Work must be referenced in the IMS with a SOW number, the work breakdown structure number, all the Measures of Effectiveness and Performance, and—most of all—a reference to the risks, which are described in the Risk Register. The IMS must indicate if these risks are being "retired" with specific work activities.

> **Not using the IMS as a "game plan" for the project team.** Without it, the team members don't know what work they are accountable for, when that work is to be performed, what the outcomes of that work look like, and, most important, who they are dependent on and who depends on them for products from the project. While specifically not an IMS development issue, the IMS must be "usable" during the management of the project. This means the IMS must be treated as a piece of literature—readable, understandable, unambiguous, not confusing to the project team, and most of all having the integrity needed to make management decisions.

Risk Management Plan

The best way to think about risk management is to reflect on Tim Lister's advice: "Risk management is how adults manage projects."[6] Risk management is essential to the success of any significant project. Information about key project cost, performance, and schedule attributes is often unknown until the project is under way. These risks can be mitigated, reduced, or retired with a risk management process. Risk management is concerned with the outcomes of a future event, the impacts of which are unknown.[7] Risk management is about dealing with this uncertainty.

In Chapter 3, we discussed how to perform Continuous Risk Management. Now, let's look at the motivation for this process and the beneficial outcomes it produces. Five simple concepts of risk management are represented in the Risk Register and the Risk Management Plan:

1. **Hope is not a strategy.** Hoping that something positive happens will not lead to success. Preparing for success is the basis of success. We need a written plan for identifying and handling the risks that threaten the success of the project. This is the basis of the Risk Management Plan. If it is not written down, it will not be handled.

2. **All single-point estimates are wrong.** Single-point estimates of cost, schedule, and technical performance are no better than 50/50 guesses in the absence of knowledge about the variances of the underlying distribution. In our Risk Management Plan, we must have credible estimates for our work and the performance of the outcomes from the work. This means a probabilistic estimate of cost and schedule at a minimum. With these estimates, we can plan for the contingencies needed to deliver on-time and on-budget.

3. **Without integrating cost, schedule, and technical performance, we are looking in the rearview mirror.** The effort to produce the product or service and the resulting value cannot be made without making these connections. Our Risk Management Plan must describe how we are going to integrate these three elements and state who is accountable for ensuring that they are properly connected to show not only the risks, but also how they will be handled.

4. **Without a model for risk management, you are driving in the dark with the headlights turned off.** Risk management is not an ad hoc process that you can make up as you go along. A formal foundation for risk management is needed. Choose one that

has worked in high-risk domains, such as defense, nuclear power, or manned spaceflight.

5. **Risk communication is everything.** Identifying risks without communicating them is a waste of time. The Risk Management Plan must include a Risk Communication Plan that connects the project participants with the customer so all the risks are visible, are agreed upon, and have acceptable handling plans in place.

To be credible, the Risk Management Plan must contain the following four sections:

1. **Executive Summary.** A short summary of the project and the risks associated with the activities of the project. Each risk needs an ordinal rank, a planned mitigation for any active risks, and approval by the Risk Board, which is accountable for reviewing and approving the risks. Once approved, the Risk Board reviews progress to retiring or handling the risks and confirms that the risks are not growing or new risks have not been recognized. The mitigation plans are then included in the IMS with their costs defined and approved.

2. **Project Description.** A detailed description of the project and the risk associated with each of the deliverables. Each of the descriptions needs to speak to what happens if the risk occurs, how it is going to be prevented from happening, the probabilities of it happening, and residual probability of the risk after the mitigation work has been done. This residual risk probability is always there, because in the project management world, there is no such thing as anything being 100 percent certain.

3. **Risk Reduction Activities by Phase.** Using a formal risk management process that connects risk, mitigation, and the IMS. The efforts for mitigation need to appear in the schedule.

4. **Risk Management Methodology.** The risk management process, as shown in Figure 3.3, is a good place start. This approach is proven and approved for use in high-risk, high-reward projects. The steps in the process are not optional and should be executed for ALL risk processes.

The Risk Register

The Risk Management Plan tells us how we are going to manage risks on the project. The Risk Register is where we record these risks, their probability of occurrence and impacts, and our handling strategy. Figure 7.2 shows a hypothetical Risk Register for our kitchen remodel project, showing the minimum number of elements needed to manage project risks. Risk is composed of two core components:

1. **The "Threat."** Circumstances with the potential to produce a loss or harm the project in some way.

2. **The "Consequences."** The loss that will occur when the threat is realized.

There are three ways to structure the risk statement in the Risk Register, but they always contain the same syntax:

1. **An If-Then Statement.** "If we miss our next milestone, then the project will fail to achieve its production, cost, and schedule objectives."

2. **A Conditions-Concern Statement.** "Data indicate that some tasks are behind schedule and staffing levels may be inadequate. We are concerned the program could fail to achieve its production, cost, and schedule objectives."

FIGURE 7.2 Risk Register.

ID	Risk Description	Likelihood	Impact	Handling Plan
1	Internal wiring not sufficient to handle new appliance load	75%	Medium	Go to county and pull original drawings for main panel. Perform "max load" test on main panel. If insufficient capacity, install secondary panel in basement.
2	Range exhaust hood flow obstructed	50%	High	Cut into ceiling wallboard to determine direction of floor joists.
3	Floor load insufficient for built-in appliances	50%	High	Model the load of built-ins and engineer loading plates before ordering.

3. **A Condition-Event-Consequence Statement.** "Data indicate that some tasks are behind schedule and staffing levels may be inadequate (condition). This will mean (event) missing our next milestone, with the project (consequence) failing to achieve its production, cost, and schedule objectives."

The Risk Register must contain descriptions of the risk, impact, consequences, and conditions before any risk-handling plans can be made. Simply making a list of risks is not sufficient to protect the project from their occurrence.

The next step is to rank the risks so we can prioritize them, along with their impacts and cost to "handle." In Performance-Based Project Management, risks need to be defined in terms of "cardinal" measures,[8] that is, measures that are "calibrated" to the domain of the risk.[9] The ordinal risk measure is just a relative ranking of the risks—one risk is higher rank than another. The cardinal risk measure is a numeric value describing the specific impact on the project in term of cost, schedule, or technical performance. For example, an A-level cardinal risk will have a 15 percent unfavorable impact on cost and a 20 percent unfavorable impact on schedule.

The details of this cardinal approach are described on a scale of A, B, C, D, E, and each of these values is assigned specific probabilities of occurrence. For example, the probability of occurrence in cardinal terms might be expressed as:

> ➤ A = unlikely to occur = 10 percent probability of occurrence

> ➤ E = highly likely to occur = 90 percent probability of occurrence

The impacts require more detail about what will actually happen, and might be expressed as:

> ➤ A = minimal or no impact

> ➤ B = minor reduction in technical capability

> ➤ E = severe degradation of the technical performance

These cardinal values can then be used to construct a Risk Register like the one shown in Figure 7.3.

FIGURE 7.3 Example of a Risk Register.

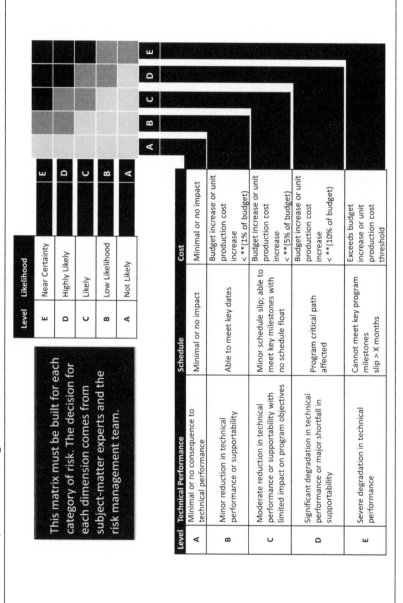

Level	Likelihood
E	Near Certainty
D	Highly Likely
C	Likely
B	Low Likelihood
A	Not Likely

This matrix must be built for each category of risk. The decision for each dimension comes from subject-matter experts and the risk management team.

Level	Technical Performance	Schedule	Cost
A	Minimal or no consequence to technical performance	Minimal or no impact	Minimal or no impact
B	Minor reduction in technical performance or supportability	Able to meet key dates	Budget increase or unit production cost increase < **(1% of budget)
C	Moderate reduction in technical performance or supportability with limited impact on program objectives	Minor schedule slip; able to meet key milestones with no schedule float	Budget increase or unit production cost increase < **(5% of budget)
D	Significant degradation in technical performance or major shortfall in supportability	Program critical path affected	Budget increase or unit production cost increase < **(10% of budget)
E	Severe degradation in technical performance	Cannot meet key program milestones slip > X months	Exceeds budget increase or unit production cost threshold

Performance Measurement Baseline

The Performance Measurement Baseline may seem redundant, but it is the primary assessment tool for assuring the credibility of the project's plan. It is the baseline of the cost, schedule, and deliverables for each work activity. Four activities must be done to produce a PMB:

1. **Identify the business needs by describing the required business capabilities.** These capabilities transcend simple features and function. They are the capabilities required by the business to meet its strategic objectives. The outcome of this effort is:

   a. A clear and concise description for the business's needed capabilities.

   b. A description of the value stream these business capabilities enable. This value stream can be connected to the business case to close the loop for project governance.

2. **Establish a requirements baseline derived from these business capabilities.** These requirements should first be stated in business process terms, then in technical feature terms. Deconstructing these requirements is done using a requirements tree that traces to the work breakdown structure. In this way, the work packages that implement the requirements that, in turn, fulfill the needed capabilities are identified.

3. **Establish a Performance Measurement Baseline.** This is based on the work derived from the requirements baseline, and is represented in work packages that are arranged in a logical network with budgets spread across the packages of work in a time-phased manner showing the amount of budget and when that amount is needed. In some domains, budget is the same as cash. In others, this spread is a picture of cash flow. In other domains, budget and funding are separated, so this budget spread is just an indication of how much money will be consumed during the planned period of work. The "cash" for the work comes through the invoicing process.

   a. Balance the budgeted cost for the work for each work activity. Determine how much it is going to cost to deliver a capability, the requirements for that capability, and the actual deliverables that implement the requirements. This "estimate" is just that—an estimate. It does not have to be precise, nor can it be precise. But it needs to be "reasonable" and "credible." Without these estimates, the customer and the project team have no real understanding of what is ahead.

b. Balance the budget across the entire project. Examine where there is risk in the work to be performed. Develop a "management reserve" for those areas, and explicitly assign that reserve to be used to cover that risk.

c. Identify the physical percent complete measurement criteria for each deliverable. Measure only "tangible outcomes" from effort. Do not measure progress by measuring effort or cost; neither is a measurement of progress.

4. **Execute the Performance Measurement Baseline** needed to control the work by rolling up the properly spread budgets into a project-level budget assessment.

a. Capture the actual cost of work performed and physical percent complete. Both are needed to assess progress to plan. The cost of the work performed measures the cost variance: "How much should we have spent at this point in the project?" The physical percent complete measures the schedule variance. "How much physical progress should we have made at this point in the project?"

b. Make management decisions based on the performance of the project using these numbers. Compare planned versus actual for both cost and schedule. With the variances, take explicit management action for the future work to "get back to GREEN."

Three Performance Measurement Baselines

When we say Performance Measurement Baseline, there are actually three of them. Figure 6.4 shows them at the high level; here are the details:

1. The **Technical Performance Baseline** is the requirements flow down and traceability map for each deliverable in the program.

   a. A critical performance measure of the Technical Performance Baseline is the stability of requirements. The expected technical achievement for the actual progress is compared to the planned progress using periodic measurements or tests. These measures start with the Technical Performance Baseline, which defines the units of measure for a properly delivered product or service.

   b. An important aspect of the Technical Performance Baseline is defining the units of measure for each deliverable in order to know what "done" looks like at each incremental assessment of maturity.

2. The **Schedule Performance Baseline** is the sequence of the work activities that produces the products or services from the program. This baseline contains the schedule margin derived from a Monte Carlo simulation. The Monte Carlo simulation is a mechanism that constructs a sample of the durations for the work from a probability distribution of the possible duration values. Using the scheduling tools, these samples are used to compute the completing times of the deliverables. A histogram is then constructed of the "probability of occurrence" of all the possible completion times that shows. The benefit of this approach is to show the "confidence levels" for all estimates, not just the single number. With these confidence levels, the project manager can have visibility into the probability of success of delivering on time and on budget in ways not possible with just a single scalar number.

3. The **Cost Performance Baseline** is the "authorized time-phased budget-at-completion used to measure, monitor, and control overall cost performance on the program."[10]

Six Steps in Developing the Performance Measurement Baseline

Earlier chapters provided an overview of the Performance Measurement Baseline; now we will look at how that baseline is created.

1. **Deconstruct project scope.** This signifies deconstructing the project into a work breakdown structure starting with well-formed technical, business, and project requirements. *Well-formed* means the requirements are traceable to the business case. Without this connection, the necessary technical, cost, and schedule tradeoffs cannot be made in an analytical manner.

2. **Assign responsibility.** Identify those accountable for the individual work packages. All aspects of the work package are under the control of the person assigned, including the descriptive information and attributes fields. Although this seems simple, it is a critical aspect of the PMB, because without a single point of integrative responsibility the development of a credible baseline can become a vague and out-of-control process.

3. **Arrange work packages.** The resulting work packages are organized in a logical network, with predecessors and successors. No widows or orphans, no lead or lag relationships, no hard constraints (only as soon as possible).

4. **Develop time-phased budget.** Budget spreads are developed from the labor assignments with named resources and their labor rates. The work package manager is accountable for producing a *credible* budget spread for each work package.

5. **Assign performance measures.** Objective performance measures are limited to 0 percent/100 percent completion and apportioned milestones with percent assignment. The apportioned milestones must be based on physical evidence of completion and agreed to by the project manager.

6. **Set Performance Measurement Baseline.** With the budget spreads and objective performance measures in place, the network of work activities can be baselined.

Requirements Traceability Matrix

When we start to develop requirements that are derived from the needed user capabilities, the first impulse is to simply make a list of the requirements. But we actually need a Traceability Matrix in the form of a table that connects the requirements to the other artifacts of the project, starting with a map of the requirements and the needed capabilities. These requirements are traced to the needed capabilities and to the WBS. From the WBS, the requirements are traced to the work packages in the IMS. Each requirement then has a home, a reason for being—the capability; an implementation activity—the WBS and work package; a MoE; a MoP; a KPP; and a TPM. The matrix that contains this information is the guide for assessing if the deliverable is "done." This leaves no ambiguity about what "done" means.

MoEs, MoPs, KPPs, and TPMs

The terms "Measures of Effectiveness" and "Measures of Performance" are likely new terms outside the defense and space flight industries, but they are critical to determining what "done" looks like for any project. These artifacts need to be written down and agreed to by the customer and the project management team before committing to a cost and schedule. In order for requirements that fulfill the needed capabilities that must be delivered by the project to be met, we need to know in some clear and concise way how effective the outcomes must be.

In almost every project, the description of the problem to be solved is "ill-formed," with no clear criteria to guide the selection of the solution.[11] These measures are the basis for increasing the probability of the project's success, and must be established before proceeding to develop the other attributes the project requires. They state what "done" looks like in units meaningful to the decision makers. Here, we'll simply define what they mean:

> ➤ **Measures of Effectiveness (MoE).** These are operational measures of success that are closely related to the achievements of the mission or operational objectives evaluated in the operational environment under a specific set of conditions. The MoEs

focus on capabilities independent of any technical implementation. They describe what "success" means for the customer. The MoEs are "mission" or "business case" dependent and must discriminate between the choices that can be made during the development of the project's outcomes. They measure the extent to which MoPs satisfy their requirements. In the end, the MoE is a measure of the utility of the solution: Can the resulting system "do the job it is intended to do"?And if so, how will we recognize that it is doing that job? The MoE is the basis of customer satisfaction. The utility is defined by the customer. In our ERP example, effectiveness is measured by reducing the costs, but also by establishing a platform for scaling the solution to continue to reduce the cost of transaction processing over time. For our kitchen remodel, the "utility" is the look and feel of the result. This is one of those intangible benefits to the remodel that can't be "spec'd in" on the drawings. The role of the kitchen designer is to ensure that the "feel" of the result is satisfying.

> **Measures of Performance (MoP).** Characterize physical or functional attributes relating to the system's operation, measured or estimated under specific conditions. They are the attributes that ensure that the system has the capability to perform the needed functions or services. They assess the system to ensure that the design requirements satisfy the Measures of Effectiveness. For example, the MoP for an automobile might be how fast it can accelerate from zero to sixty. This is meaningful to the driver when merging into traffic on the highway. In other words, it provides some tangible evidence that the resulting product or service is fulfilling its "mission." The MoP is the way to measure what the system will achieve when it is operational.

> **Key Performance Parameters (KPP).** Represent the capabilities and characteristics so significant that failure to meet them can be cause for reevaluation, reassessment, or termination of the project. The customer gets to define the KPPs, starting with which ones are "key." The "key" KPP for the kitchen remodel will be the traffic flow for cooking work. If there are collisions all the time between the cooks in the kitchen, then the design and implementation KPP will not have been met. For the ERP

system, a KPP would be the transaction rate, but also the error rate for those transactions. Having high-transaction capacity but a high error rate does no good, because the corrections of the transaction swamp the throughput.

> **Technical Performance Measures (TPM).** Attributes that determine how well a system or system element is satisfying or expected to satisfy a technical requirement or goal. The TPMs are assigned during the design process. They define the compliance to the performance requirements of the outcomes of the project. They are the primary attribute used to describe risk, because if the TPM is not "in compliance," the outcome of the project will not be acceptable to the customer. One TPM for the ERP system is the availability of the system around the world. These "…ilities" are the starting point for TPM: reliability, sustainability, reparability, maintainability.

Looking Back

The management of projects encompasses a variety of activities such as managing cost, schedule, resources, performance assessments, and so on. But before those can be successful, we need to know what to measure, how to measure it, the units of measure, and the descriptions of what "done" looks like using those measures. In this chapter, we've examined a few—the critical few—documents needed to perform these measurements. Starting with the Statement of Work and Statement of Objectives, there is agreement on what the project should be doing to produce the outcomes the customer needs. A Concept of Operations further describes what the outcomes of the project will be "doing" when they arrive. The ConOps is the source of the Measures of Effectiveness and Measures of Performance for the project's products or services.

In order to identify what work needs to be done and what exactly will result from that work we need a work breakdown structure. The WBS tells us what deliverables will be produced and how they are related. In addition to the WBS, we need the organizational breakdown structure to know "who" is going to be doing the work to produce the "what." The Responsibility Assignment Matrix shows how these connections are made and the person "accountable" for the successful delivery of the outcomes.

With these documents in hand, we can start to build the Integrated Master Schedule to perform the work needed to produce the project's outcomes. We also need to identify the impediments to our success through the Risk Management Plan and the resulting Risk Register. Finally, all of these elements are assembled into the Performance Measurement Baseline, which is a "time-phased" cost and schedule of the work to be performed to complete the project.

In order to measure our performance, we need to know how effective we must be for success and what performance goals the project must satisfy. We can't measure everything on the project, but we need to measure the Key Performance Parameters (KPP) and the technical performance of each deliverable as the project progresses toward its goal. When all the measurement metrics are used, the customer gains visibility into the delivered capabilities that provide the business value, the technical performance that ensures that capabilities will be provided on time, on budget, and with the planned performance.

Only when all of these measures are in place, traceable to the plans and scheduling, measured using physical percent complete, and produced on time, on budget, with risks identified and handled, with all the planned resources available and ready to work can the project be considered "under control."

RECOMMENDED READING

*Knowledge is of two kinds. We know a subject ourselves, or we
know where we can find information upon it. When we enquire
into any subject, the first thing we have to do is to know what
books have treated of it. This leads us to look at catalogues,
and at the backs of books in libraries.*

Samuel Johnson (*Boswell's Life of Johnson*)

Books provide an abundant source of knowledge about how to manage
projects. All good project managers have a collection of books on their
shelves. They may have read these books, they may apply the contents
on a daily basis, or they may own many of the books for future reference. I buy books on impulse. But over time, I've learned that that impulse was usually for a reason. Books I purchased years before turn out
to be needed later.

The list that follows is, of course, not exhaustive. It is a list based on actually managing projects and reflects my "hands-on" experiences.

> *The Advanced Theory of Statistics,* Sir Maurice Kendall and Alan Stuart (MacMillan, 1977). Probability and statistics is the basis of all analysis of project performance. This is the primary source of statistical analysis.

> *Agile Project Management for Government,* Brian Wernham (Maitland & Strong, 2012). This book is a guide for deploying software in complex environments using agile methods. The case studies show it can be done. The step-by-step guidance shows you how it can be done.

> *Antipatterns in Project Management,* William J. Brown, Hays W. "Skip" McCormick III, and Scott W. Thomas (John Wiley & Sons, 2000). Brown and his co-authors describe the "anti-patterns" of poor project management. The patterns paradigm was once popular in the software development realm but is still applicable to both software and project management. In this book, you'll find anti-patterns that are likely in place on your projects today.

> *Apollo Root Cause Analysis: A New Way of Thinking,* Dean Gano (Apollonian Publications, 2003). Root cause analysis is the basis of process improvement. Without an assessment of the root causes, there is no way to determine what to fix. The fixes are simply paving over the real problem.

> *The Art of Modeling Dynamic Systems: Forecasting for Chaos, Randomness, and Determinism,* Foster Morrison (John Wiley & Sons, 1991). Modeling a project as a dynamic system is a way to make informed decisions. This book shows how to develop these models and put them to work.

> *The Art of Systems Architecting,* 2nd edition, Mark Maier and Eberhardt Rechtin (CRC Press, 2000). Rechtin essentially "invented" the analysis of "system of systems (SoS)." Nearly everything in the modern project world is a SoS. Rechtin speaks to software

systems as well as complex space, defense, and other systems. This is the basis for defining the needed capabilities I described in Chapter 3 of this book.

> ➤ *Assumption-Based Planning: A Tool for Reducing Avoidable Surprises,* James A. Dewar (Cambridge University Press, 2002). Assumptions are the basis of project success and project failure. Planning in the presence of assumptions is a fundamental process for project success.

> ➤ *Catastrophe Disentanglement: Getting Software Projects Back on Track,* E. M. Bennatan (Addison Wesley, 2006). All projects get into trouble. This book tells you how to get out of trouble.

> ➤ *Continuous Risk Management Guidebook,* Audrey J. Dorofee, et al. (Carnegie Mellon University, 1996). This is the basis of the Continuous Risk Management process. While focused on software development, CRM can be applied to any domain.

> ➤ *Effective Opportunity Management for Projects: Exploiting Positive Risk,* David Hillson (Taylor Francis, 2004). Hillson, the "Risk Doctor," writes about risk management from an integrated approach not found anywhere other than in Ed Conrow's work.

> ➤ *Effective Risk Management: Some Keys to Success,* 2nd edition, Edmund H. Conrow (AIAA, 2003). This is the seminal work on managing risk. While not written for the casual reader, Conrow's work is a mandatory read for anyone serious about risk management. A critical concept, lost on many in the project management business, including PMI, is the improper use of "cardinal" numbers to rank and classify risk. Conrow shows us that this is a serious mistake. Cardinal numbers must be used correctly. This means the values used to classify, rank, and compare risks must be "calibrated."

> ➤ *Execution: The Discipline of Getting Things Done,* Larry Bossidy and Ram Charan (Crown Business, 2002). Bossidy is a graduate of Crotonville, New York, the University of General Electric. Project

management is about "execution"—executing the right work, at the right time, with the right outcomes. This book provides the basis for how to do it.

> *The Flaw of Averages: Why We Underestimate Risk in the Face of Uncertainty,* Sam L. Savage (John Wiley & Sons, 2012). The words *estimates* and *averages* are frequently used, but often misunderstood. This book will tell you what they mean. After reading it, you'll never use these terms again without the proper qualifications.

> *Forecast Scheduling with Microsoft Project 2010: Best Practices for Real-World Projects,* Eric Uyttewaal (Project Pro, 2010). There are lots of books on managing projects using Microsoft Project. Uyttewaal's book goes far beyond the normal advice. The book has step-by-step instructions to do almost anything you need to do on the project using this tool.

> *The Handbook of Program Management: How to Facilitate Project Success with Optimal Program Management,* James T. Brown (McGraw Hill, 2008). Dr. Brown has sixteen years of experience managing NASA projects and works at the executive level of NASA. This book is a guide for developing and deploying a program management office in any domain that works with high-risk, high-value projects.

> *How NASA Builds Teams: Mission Critical Soft Skills for Scientists, Engineers, and Project Teams,* Charles J. Pellerin (John Wiley & Sons, 2009). Projects are managed by teams. This book describes how NASA builds teams.

> *How to Think About Statistics,* John Phillips (Freeman, 1996). In discussions of statistics, we are frequently told how the numbers are used to manipulate outcomes. This book provides guidance on how to apply statistics and interpret the outcomes of statistical analysis.

> *Introduction to Probability Models,* 4th edition, Sheldon M. Ross (Academic Press, 1989). If we're going to build probabilistic models

of how project elements interact, we need to provide a foundation for them. This book can help us do it.

> *Little Bets: How Breakthrough Ideas Emerge from Small Discoveries,* Peter Sims (Free Press, 2011). Often, books about agile development focus on the many paradigms built around developing "value" and the processes needed to develop that value. This book provides a much larger picture of the business processes.

> *The Management of Projects,* Peter W. G. Morris (Thomas Telford Publishing, 1997). Dr. Morris is a professor of Project Management at the University of Manchester, Institute of Science and Technology. Morris's books have guided the development of project management processes in construction and information technology. This book provides a historical perspective of project management as the basis for developing improvements.

> *Managing Risk: Methods for Software Systems Development,* Elaine M. Hall, SEI Series in Software Engineering (Addison Wesley, 1998). There are many risk management books and articles. Many are good; some are not. This is a good book for software projects. (You'll find others on this list as well.)

> *The Martian Principles for Successful Enterprise Systems: 20 Lessons Learned from NASA's Mars Exploration Rover Mission,* Ronald Mak (John Wiley & Sons, 2006). In discussions about agile development or emergent requirements, we rarely speak about a specific problem domain. This book does. The problem domain is designing, building, and "flying" a Mars landing machine in the presence of emerging everything.

> *Mathematics for Dynamic Modeling,* Edward Beltrami (Academic Press, 1987). Modeling project performance means creating mathematical models of how the project elements interact and how random (stochastic) processes drive this interaction. This book is the starting point for building credible models.

> *Measuring Time: Improving Project Performance Using Earned Value Management,* Mario Vanhoucke (Springer,

2009). Vanhooucke works at the University of Ghent, where he is head of the Department of Information Science and Operations.

> ***Modelling Complex Projects,*** Terry Williams (John Wiley & Sons, 2002). Williams is a professor and heads the Management Science Department, Strathclyde University. This book describes how and when to use modeling to develop estimates, monitor and control projects, and analyze their performance, leading to successful implementations.

> ***Notes on the Synthesis of Form,*** Christopher Alexander (Harvard University Press, 1964). Early in the development of computer software, there was a connection with patterns and functionality. This is the first book that made the connection.

> ***Performance-Based Earned Value,*** Paul J. Solomon and Ralph R. Young (John Wiley & Sons, 2007). Paul J. Solomon is a colleague. He was the "performance manager" for the B-2 Flight Avionics. He was the first to carry the banner for integrating Technical Performance Measures with Earned Value Management.

> ***The Program Management Office: Establishing, Managing, and Growing the Value of a PMO,*** Craig J. Letavec (J. Ross, 2006). The notion of a program management office (PMO) is not new. Making the PMO work effectively is harder than it looks. Here's a book that can be the basis of a successful PMO.

> ***Project Management and Methods,*** Sven Antvik and Håkan Sjöholm (Projektkonsult Håkan Sjöholm AB, 2007). Sven Antvik has worked in the Swedish Defense Materiel Administration and written about his experiences and how those can improve the performance of high-risk projects.

> ***Project Management the Agile Way: Making It Work in the Enterprise,*** John C. Goodpasture (J. Ross, 2010). John Goodpasture's book shows how to integrate agile development processes with standard project development. His advice comes from hands-on experience in government and commercial organizations.

> *Radical Elements of Radical Success,* Dan Ward (Rogue Press, 2005). Colonel Ward writes about managing projects in a unique and informative way. His focus is on seeking the simplest approach to the problem.

> *Reinventing Project Management: The Diamond Approach to Successful Growth and Innovation,* Aaron Shenhar and Dov Dvir (Harvard Business School Press, 2007). This book offers a step-by-step process for managing IT projects and should be on the shelf of anyone who works in the IT business.

> *Rethinking Performance Measurement: Beyond the Balanced Scorecard,* Marshall W. Meyer (Cambridge University Press, 2002). When we speak about performance measurement, we usually start with cost, schedule, or some technical performance measure. Rarely are these measures connected to the business performance measures. And even when they are, the business performance measures are usually not connected to the "mission" of the end user. This book speaks to this issue.

> *The Seven Secrets of How to Think Like a Rocket Scientist,* Jim Longuski (Copernicus Books, 2007). We've all heard the expression, "This isn't rocket science." This is the book to go to if you want to know what it really means.

> *Software Engineering Risk Management,* Dale Walter Karolak (IEEE Computer Society, 1996). There are lots of books on risk management; this one focuses on software development risk management.

> *Software Requirements: Analysis and Specifications,* Alan Davis (Prentice-Hall, 1990). Requirements elicitation is the second of the Five Immutable Practices of project success, Chapter 3 of this book. There are many approaches to eliciting requirements; this book is a good starting point.

> *Strategic Performance Management: Leveraging and Measuring Your Intangible Value Drivers,* Bernard Marr (Elsevier, 2006). The needed capabilities I described in the discussion of the Five

Practices in Chapter 3 of this book start with a strategy for business or mission success. Managing the strategic processes is a critical success factor, and this book starts you down that road.

> *Time Series,* Sir Maurice Kendall (Hodder Arnold, 1990). All project data are a function of time. Analyzing the time series of the data can provide forecasts of future performance. This is a primary source book for that analysis.

> *A Treatise on Probability,* John Maynard Keynes (Watchmaker Publishing, 1921; reprinted 2007). This is one of the first books about probabilistic modeling. Although its focus is on economics, the principles are applicable to project management.

> *Visual Project Management: Models and Frameworks for Mastering Complex Systems,* Kevin Forsberg, Hal Mooz, and Howard Cotterman (John Wiley & Sons, 2005). The Center for Systems Management is where these authors work. It is a think tank and a practical applications source for managing complex projects and programs. This book describes their process for successfully delivering value to customers. One of their steps is "process cycles," and that is where this book connects to mine.

NOTES

CHAPTER 1: The Ten Drivers of Project Success

1. David Cleland and H. Kerzner, *A Project Management Dictionary of Terms* (New York: Van Nostrand, 1985), p. 187.

2. Max Wideman, *First Principles of Project Management*, http://www.maxwideman.com/papers/principles/principles.pdf.

3. The notion of capabilities-based planning originated in the defense domain. The Joint Requirements Oversight Council (JROC) in the U.S. Department of Defense defines the needed capabilities of equipment and services. In the IT domain, it is rare to speak about needed capabilities. Instead, projects usually start with requirements, without any knowledge about how the project's outcome will support a needed business capability.

4. Coupling and cohesion is a critical attribute of the capabilities and the requirements that result. Two components are loosely coupled when changes in one never or rarely result in a change in the other. A component exhibits high cohesion when all its capabilities are

strongly related in terms of another capability. The higher cohesion and the lower coupling a system, a design, or a function has, the more robust are its capabilities in the presence of change and the more flexible are the individual components to the same change.

5. *Implementing Capabilities Based Planning Within the Public Safety and Security Sector: Lessons from Defence Experience,* DRDC Centre for Security Science, DRDC CSS TM 2011-26, December 2011.

6. James A. Dewar, *Assumption-Based Planning: A Tool for Reducing Avoidable Surprises* (Cambridge: Cambridge University Press, 2002).

7. Ralph R. Young, *The Requirements Engineering Handbook* (Norwood, MA: Artech House, 2003).

8. I. F. Hooks and K. A. Farry, *Customer-Centered Products: Creating Successful Products Through Smart Requirements Management* (New York: AMACOM, 2001).

9. Jeffrey O. Grady, *Systems Requirements Analysis* (New York: McGraw-Hill, 1993).

10. Michael G. Christel and Kyo C. Kang, "Issues with Requirements Elicitation," Technical Report, CMU/SEI–92–TR–12, Software Engineering Institute, Carnegie Mellon University, Pittsburgh, PA 15213.

11. Ian Sommerville and Pete Sawyer, *Requirements Engineering: A Good Practice Guide* (New York: John Wiley & Sons, 1997).

12. Garry Roedler and Cheryl Jones, Technical Measurement: A Collaborative Project of PSM, INCOSE, and Industry, INCOSE-TP-2003-020-01, pp. 9–10.

13. The notion of a big, visible chart has been around for some time. These types of charts hung in the hallways of TRW, 1 Space Park, Redondo Beach, California, in the late 1970s. They were produced to show the process flow of the program, the master schedule, and who was late in delivering their outcomes to the satellite we were building. Recently, the agile software development community has been using this term. It also is a concept used in the eXtreme Programming World: "…by putting this chart in the public area, everybody gets a reminder

of where the team is on this, and visual feedback of the team's progress," http://c2.com/cgi/wiki?BigVisibleChart.

14. Charts on the wall are very effective ways to communicate complex ideas about the project. The size and visibility of these charts provide accountability to the stakeholders, focus the team on the right things, and convey a sense of urgency.

15. The discussion in this chapter is the basis of Earned Value Management. In later chapters, Earned Value Management is explained in more detail. For now, this will serve as an introduction to the concept of measuring project performance by integrating cost, schedule, and the technical performance of the products or services produced by the work efforts.

Chapter 2: The Five Immutable Principles of Project Success

1. See the Standish Reports for IT, the Government Accountability Office (GAO) reports on high risk and troubled programs, and the construction industry annual reports on project performance.

2. Mr. Blaise Durante retired from the Air Force in October 2012. He was a member of the Senior Executive Service, and is currently deputy assistant secretary for acquisition integration, Office of the Assistant Secretary of the Air Force for Acquisition, Washington, D.C. He directed the development of weapon system acquisition policy, including program direction.

3. American Baseball Coaches Association, *Practice Perfect Baseball*, Bob Bennett, ed. (Champagne, IL: Human Kinetics, 2009).

4. Susie White, *10 Principles of Garden Design* (London: Vivays Publishing, February 2012).

5. Noel Sproles, "Formulating the Measures of Effectiveness," *Systems Engineering*, 5, no. 2 (2002).

6. Frederick P. Brooks Jr., "No Silver Bullet—Essence and Accident in Software Engineering" (Chapel Hill: University of North Carolina, 1986), p. 13. http://faculty.salisbury.edu/~xswang/Research/Papers/SERelated/no-silver-bullet.pdf.

7. James A Dewar, *Assumptions-Based Planning: A Tool for Reducing Avoidable Surprises* (Cambridge: Cambridge University Press, 2002).

8. Arnoud De Meyer, Christoph H. Loch and Michael T. Pich, "Managing Project Uncertainty: From Variation to Chaos," *MIT Sloan Management Review* (Winter 2000). http://sloanreview.mit.edu/article/managing-project-uncertainty-from-variation-to-chaos/.

9. Christopher Alberts, Audrey Dorofee, "Mission Risk Diagnostic (MRD) Method Description," February 2012, TECHNICAL NOTE, CMU/SEI-2012-TN-005, http://www.sei.cmu.edu/reports/12tn005.pdf.

10. This quote is attributed to Kent Beck, *Extreme Programming Explained: Embrace Change* (Reading, MA: Addison-Wesley Professional; U.S. ed., 1999).

11. The Concept of Operations is a document describing the characteristics of a proposed system from the point of view of an individual who will use that system. It is used to communicate the quantitative and qualitative system characteristics to all stakeholders. A ConOps generally evolves from a concept and describes how a set of capabilities may be employed to achieve desired objectives or end state.

CHAPTER 3: The Five Immutable Practices of Project Success

1. Technical Performance Measures (TPM) are attributes used to determine how well a system or subsystem element is satisfying or expected to satisfy a technical requirement of a goal. Selection of TPMs should be limited to critical technical threshold or parameters that if not met put the project's cost, schedule, and performance

at risk. Garry Roedler and Cheryl Jones, *Technical Measurement: A Collaborative Project of PSM, INCOSE, and Industry,* INCOSE-TP-2003-020-01, pp. 9–10.

2. Key Performance Parameters (KPP) are critical subsets of the performance parameters representing those capabilities and characteristics so significant that failure to meet the threshold value of performance can be cause for the concept or the system to be reevaluated or the project to be reassessed or terminated. Each KPP has a threshold and objective value. KPPs are the minimum number of performance parameters needed to characterize the major drivers of operational performance, supportability, and operability. Garry Roedler and Cheryl Jones, *Technical Measurement: A Collaborative Project of PSM, INCOSE, and Industry,* INCOSE-TP-2003-020-01, p. 11.

3. Michael G. Christel and Kyo C. Kang, "Issues in Requirements Elicitation," Technical Report CMU/SEI-92-TR-012, September 1992, Software Engineering Institute, Carnegie Mellon University, Pittsburgh, PA 15213. This paper describes the critical failings of how we elicit requirements and how these failings set the stage for project failure.

4. The ConOps idea is very close to the standard use case and scenario approach developed by Alistair Cockburn, several years ago. Alistair Cockburn, *Writing Effective Use Cases* (Reading, MA: Addison-Wesley, 2000), http://www.amazon.com/Writing-Effective-Cases-Alistair-Cockburn/dp/0201702258.

5. MAJ Mark W. Brantley, USA, LTC Willie J. McFadden, USA, and LTC Mark J. Davis, USA (Ret), "Expanding the Trade Space: An Analysis of Requirements Tradeoffs Affecting System Design," *Acquisition Review Quarterly* (Winter 2002).

6. Ralph R. Young, *The Requirements Engineering Handbook* (Norwood, MA: Artech House, 2003).

7. Michael G. Christel and Kyo C. Kang, Technical Report, "Issues with Requirements Elicitation," CMU/SEI–92–TR–12, Software Engineering Institute, Carnegie Mellon University, Pittsburgh, PA 15213.

8. Paired comparison analysis, Borda ranking, and Analytical Hierarchical Process are all ways to mathematically rank comparisons of information for decision making. This approach should be used for any prioritization, ranking, or selection among choices.

9. Peter Sims, *Little Bets: How Breakthrough Ideas Emerge from Small Discoveries* (New York: Free Press, 2011).

10. In later chapters, we'll look in detail at reference class forecasting because it is a powerful approach not only for forecasting but also for addressing the anchoring and adjustment processes needed to produce credible estimates and identify risks and their mitigations. Reference class forecasting is used in oil and gas industries, NASA, and Defense Department cost and schedule estimating processes. We will apply it to our sample projects.

11. Audrey J. Dorofee, Julie A. Walker, Christopher J. Alberts, Ronald P. Higuere, Richard L. Murphy, and Ray C, Williams, *Continuous Risk Management Guidebook* (Pittsburgh, PA: Carnegie Mellon University, Software Engineering Institute, 1996).

12. David P. Gluch, *A Construct for Describing Software Development Risk*, CMU/SEI-94-TR-14, ADA284922, Carnegie Mellon University, 1994.

CHAPTER 4: The Five Governing Processes of Project Management

1. Peter Weill and Jeanne W. Ross, *IT Governance: How Top Performers Manage IT Decision Rights for Superior Results* (Cambridge, MA: Harvard Business School Press, 2004).

2. Aaron J. Shenhar and Dov Dvir, *Reinventing Project Management: The Diamond Approach to Successful Growth and Innovation* (Cambridge, MA: Harvard Business School Press, 2007).

3. Ibid.

4. Shenhar, et al., "Project Success: A Multidimensional Strategic Concept," *Long Range Planning* 34, no. 6 (December 2001), pp. 699–725.

5. If you wish to read more about governance processes, a good place to start is the reference books by Weill and Ross. Another is the Balanced Scorecards for projects.

6. J. Gido and J. P. Clements, *Successful Project Management* (Cincinnati, OH: South-Western College Pub., 1999).

7. Eric Norman, Shelly Brotherton, and Robert Fried, *Work Breakdown Structures: The Foundation for Project Management Excellence* (Hoboken, NJ: Wiley, 2008).

8. "Total Cost Management Framework: An Integrated Approach to Portfolio, Program, and Project Management," AACE International, 2006.

9. In defense contracting, MIL-STD-881C defines how the work breakdown structure should be built.

10. *A Guide to the Project Management Body of Knowledge* (*PMBOK*® *Guide*)—Fourth Edition, An American National Standard ANSI/PMI 99-001-2008 (Newtown Square, PA: Project Management Institute, Inc., 2008).

11. Thomas C. Powell, "Strategic Planning as Competitive Advantage," *Strategic Management*, 13, no. 7 (October 1992), pp. 551–558.

12. This person is called a control account manager. The control account has a budget, a period of performance, assigned resources, and a detailed description of the work to be performed during that period of performance. The summation of all the budgets in the control accounts equals the Performance Measurement Baseline budget for the project. Management Reserve is outside of this budget, since Management Reserve is not assigned to actual work.

13. The concept of a "single point of integrative responsibility," can be found in introductory managerial finance books, such as Scott Besley and Eugene Brigham, *Essentials of Managerial Finance*. This single point of responsibility does not occur when there is shared ownership, which results in confusion about the status of the project.

14. Milestones have to be used with care. In ancient Rome, the Emperor Augustus placed a gilded pillar at the center of the Forum, the Millarium Aureum. This marked the starting point for a system of roads, all of which led to Rome. Every mile (*mille*— Latin for 1,000— the distance a Roman Legion covered in 1,000 paces) of road was marked with a stone "millarium" or milestone. The milestones had several purposes. In our project paradigm, milestones should not be just rocks on the side of the road that we look at as we pass— rather, they should have tangible meaning.

15. Douglas Adams, English humorist and science fiction novelist (1952–2001), best known for his *Hitchhiker's Guide to the Galaxy*.

Chapter 5: Project Management Execution

1. Lean construction is a method of incrementally developing the constructed outcome using the principles of "Agile." http://www.leanconstruction.org/.

Chapter 6: Tailoring the Principles and Practices for Project Success

1. Curtis R. Cook, Ph.D., "Project Management in Research and Development," Energy Contractors Group (EFCOG), Project Management Working Group, 2010. PMP, *Just Enough Project Management* (New York: The McGraw Hill Companies, Inc., 2005).

2. *Mutually exclusive* means two events or conditions cannot occur at the same time. *Collectively exhaustive* means at least one of the events or requirements must be present. The concept of MECE comes from Ethan Rasiel and Paul Friga, *The McKinsey Mind: Understanding and Implementing the Problem-Solving Tools and Management Techniques of the World's Top Strategic Consulting Firm* (New

York: McGraw-Hill, 2001). This concept is a "rule" for assessing requirements. It is not a product unto itself. The lack of overlap means there is no confusion among the elements of the requirements. No gap means nothing is left out.

3. RACI is responsible, accountable, consulted, and informed. Responsible are those doing the work to achieve the outcomes. Accountable are those ultimately answerable for the correct and thorough completion of the deliverable or task and the one who delegates the work to those responsible. Consulted are typically subject-matter experts. Informed are those who are kept up-to-date on progress, usually on completion of the task or deliverable from the work packages.

4. *Separation of concerns* is a computer science term that is applicable to projects as well. It means dividing the activities of the project into distinct sections, minimizing the coupling between these sections, and maximizing the cohesion of the sections within the overall project. The value of this approach is the simplification of the management processes. Work is "coupled" at the interfaces only. Cohesion is maintained across the boundaries between the sections so all the participants have a clear and concise understanding of what products are to be produced, what their measures of performance are, and who is accountable for the delivery and the performance.

5. *Coupling* and *cohesion* are also computer science terms. *Coupling* describes the relationships between "objects" and *cohesion* describes the relationships with "objects." In our case, these "objects" are the work packages and their products or services. We want to maximize the cohesion within the collection of work packages, so everyone working on the same capability and the requirements for that capability are "on the same page" about what "done" looks like. We want to minimize the coupling between work packages or groups of work packages to minimize the impact of poor performance in one set of work packages on other sets of work packages.

CHAPTER 7: Deliverables Needed for Project Management Success

1. Office of Management, Budget, and Evaluation, *Project Management Practices Rev E,* June 2003, US Department of Energy, Work Breakdown Structure.

2. Ibid.

3. Ibid.

4. Ibid.

5. Ibid.

6. Tim Lister is a fellow of the Cutter Business Technology Council and Business Technology Strategies practice and a senior consultant with Cutter's Agile Product & Project Management and Government & Public Sector practices. Tim coined the phrase "Risk Management is how adults manage projects" in a presentation at the Boston SPIN (Software Process Improvement Network), http://www.boston-spin.org/slides/039-Jan2004-talk.pdf. This quote can be the basis of everything you do around risk management.

7. Arnoud De Meyer, Christoph H. Loch, and Michael T. Pich, "Managing Project Uncertainty: From Variation to Chaos," *MIT Sloan Management Review* (Winter 2002).

8. Many books and papers guide us in assigning numbers to the probability of something occurring and then ranking the risks using those numbers. They also guide use in assigning numbers to the impact. The two numbers are then multiplied together to get a risk score. This approach, called ordinal ranking, must be avoided if we are to have a credible Risk Management Plan. "Ordinal" ranking is a relative comparison of two items. "This risk is larger than that risk, because one has a 1 assigned and the other has a 2 assigned."

9. Louis Anthony Cox, "What's Wrong with Risk Matrices?" *Society of Risk Management* (2008), pp. 497–512.

10. This paradigm comes from the federal government's acquisition processes. The starting point for information about this and other program management topics is https://dap.dau.mil/acquipedia/ Pages/Default.aspx.

11. Philip M. Morse and George E. Kimball, *Methods of Operations Research* (Los Altos, CA: Peninsula Publishing, 1970).

INDEX